To

From

Date

VeggieTales

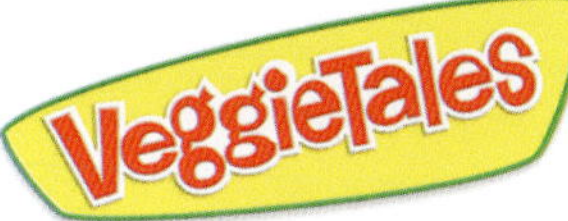

GOD IS MY FRIEND

365 Daily Devos for Girls

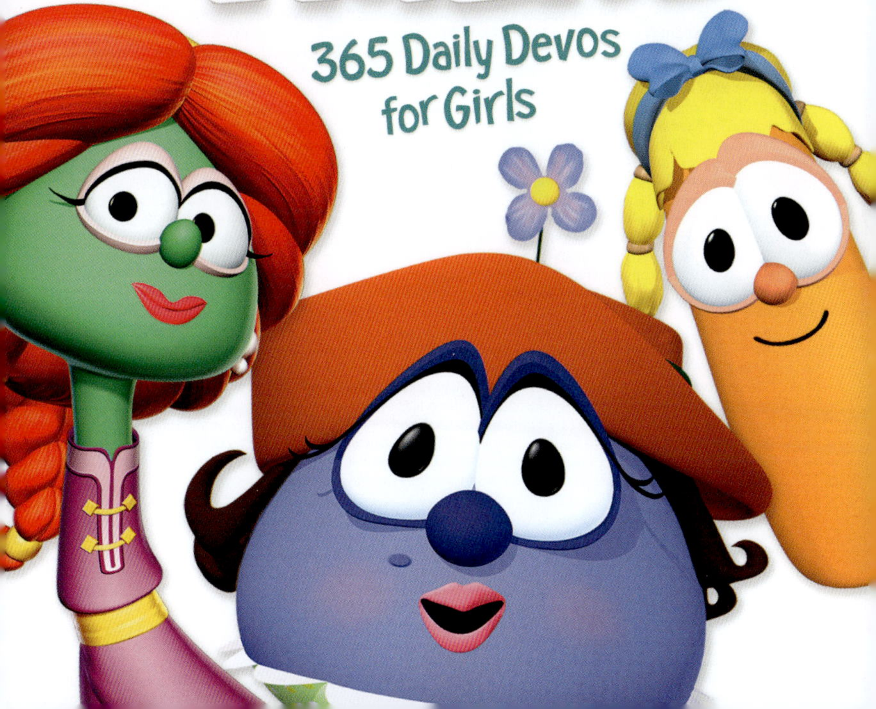

ISBN: 978-1-5460-0870-5 (paperback)
ISBN: 978-1-5460-0871-2 (padded hardcover)

WorthyKids
Hachette Book Group
1290 Avenue of the Americas, New York, NY 10104

Distributed in the United Kingdom by Hachette UK Ltd., Carmelite House, 50 Victoria Embankment, London, EC4Y 0DZ

Distributed in Europe by Hachette Livre, 58 rue Jean Bluezen, 92 178 Vanves Cedex, France

WorthyKids is a division of Hachette Book Group, Inc. The WorthyKids name and logo are trademarks of Hachette Book Group, Inc.

Printed and bound in Dongguan, China
APS • 06/25
10 9 8 7 6 5 4 3 2 1

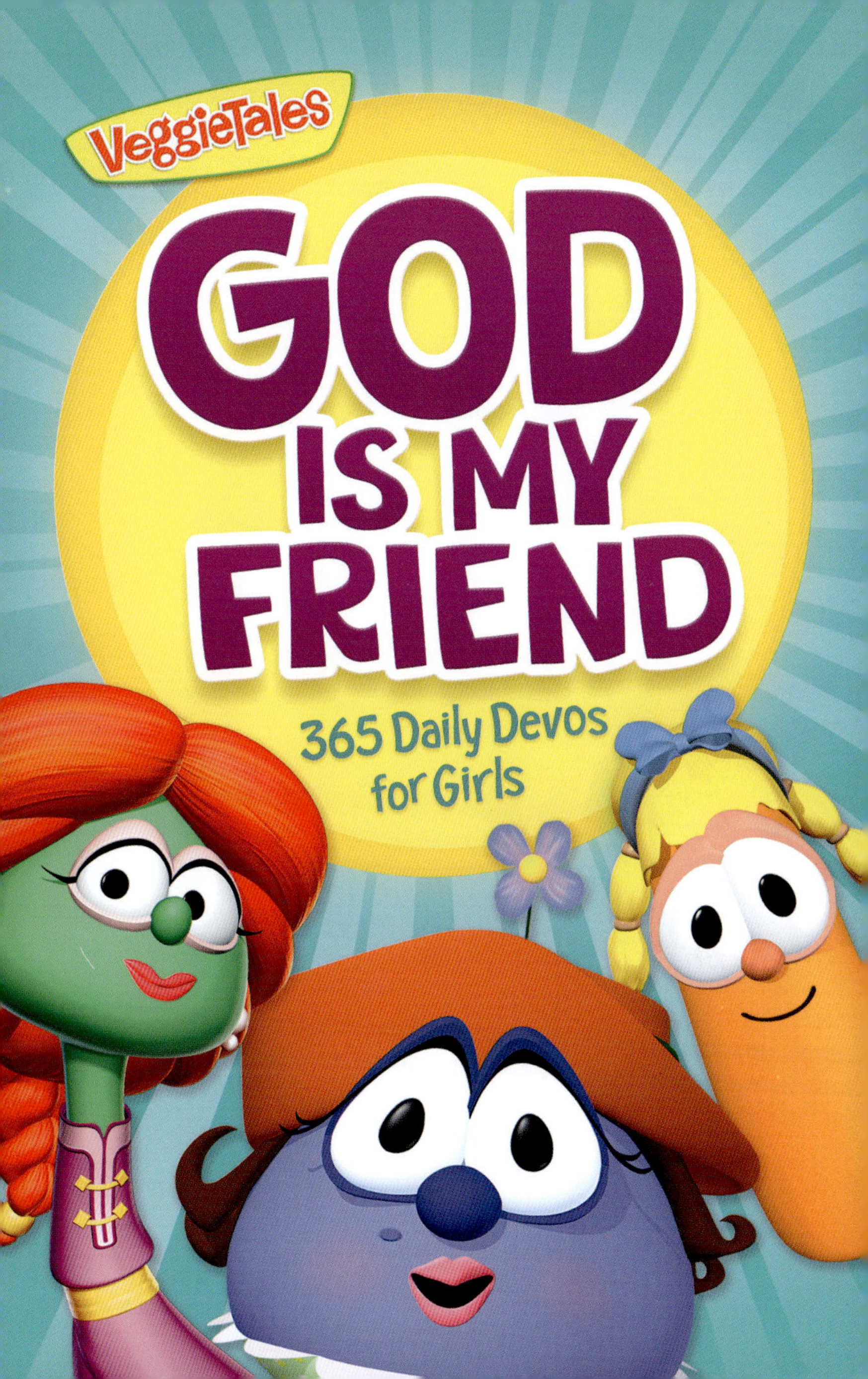
VeggieTales
GOD IS MY FRIEND
365 Daily Devos for Girls

A NOTE TO PARENTS OR GRANDPARENTS

As a parent or grandparent, you know the importance of teaching children the big ideas that are found in God's Word and encouraging them to spend time with Him. The daily devotions in this book will help you do that.

Each entry contains a Bible verse and a kid-friendly devotion on an important topic such as honesty, forgiveness, or kindness. A question or thought follows to reinforce the message for the day, and a daily prayer will help your child to develop a habit of talking to God.

During the coming year, encourage your daughter or granddaughter to read a devotion from this book every day. This will help her establish a daily practice of hearing from God. It will also provide 365 opportunities to share God's love and wisdom and a daily chance for her to be reminded that God made her special—He knows her so well and loves her very much.

LIVE IN LOVE

"As the Father has loved Me, I have also loved you. Remain in My love."

JOHN 15:9 HCSB

Jesus came to earth to show us what God's love looks like. Just look at any Jesus story you know! He cares for everyone, no matter who they are or what they have done. He listens when His friends ask questions and share worries. He is patient and gentle, and He stands up for those who are hurt or left out.

But He doesn't just show us God's love. He tells us to live in it! When you remember God's love and show it to others, you'll always stay close to God. And that's a great place to be!

THOUGHT OF THE DAY

Read a Jesus story today. Can you find God's love in it?

PRAY TODAY

Dear God, what amazing love You have! Help me always remember it, and share it with others too! Amen.

BE A GENTLE HELPER

Are there those among you who are truly wise and understanding? Then they should show it by living right and doing good things with a gentleness that comes from wisdom.

JAMES 3:13 NCV

When you can do something well, it is fun and easy for you. Are you good at music or sports or math? When we are good at something, we might brag, show off, or think we are better than others. We might say, "Why can't you do that? It's SO easy." But what's easy for you isn't always easy for others.

Instead, be kind! Knowing how to do something well gives you a chance to help and encourage someone else. The Bible says it's wise to be gentle. Showing off or bragging hurts others, but being gentle helps them.

THOUGHT OF THE DAY

What is something you do well? How can you gently help someone else learn to do it too?

PRAY TODAY

Dear God, thank You for giving me talents and abilities to do some things well. Please show me ways to gently help others. Amen.

HELP FOR YOU

"If you'll hold on to me for dear life," says God, "I'll get you out of any trouble. I'll give you the best of care if you'll only get to know and trust me. Call me and I'll answer, be at your side in bad times."

PSALM 91:14-15A MSG

Here's a secret: No person is perfect. Everyone makes bad choices sometimes—even grown-ups! It doesn't feel great when we make those mistakes, does it? But God has wonderful news for everyone. He will never, ever leave us! He is always working in our hearts, teaching us to love better, share more, and make kinder choices. And He loves when you ask Him for help. So next time you start worrying about a mistake, pray instead. Ask God to show you how to make things right and how to make a different choice next time.

THOUGHT OF THE DAY

No mistake can keep us away from God's love.

PRAY TODAY

Dear God, I'm so glad You never leave me. Help me remember to ask for Your help when I'm in trouble. Amen.

A MESSAGE FROM GOD

"Fear not, for I am with you; Be not dismayed, for I am your God. I will strengthen you."

ISAIAH 41:10A NKJV

Isaiah was one of God's prophets, a man who gave God's messages to His people. One very important message God wanted Isaiah to share was that no matter what happened, God would always be with His people and give them strength. Even though Isaiah delivered this message thousands of years ago, it is still true today. Remember this message when you feel worried, alone, or unsure about what to do: Don't be afraid. God is with you. He will give you strength! That is God's message for you!

THOUGHT OF THE DAY

When you don't know what to do, remember God is there with you!

PRAY TODAY

Dear God, thank You for promising to always be with me and to give me strength. Amen.

BE A GIVER

"Give, and you will receive. Your gift will return to you in full—pressed down, shaken together to make room for more, running over, and poured into your lap. The amount you give will determine the amount you get back."

LUKE 6:38 NLT

How do you feel when someone gives you something or shares with you? Doesn't it make you want to share with them too? Good friends know that being a giver not only makes others happy, it makes the giver happy too! How can you be a giver? You can help some-one learn something. You can share a snack or toy. You can draw a picture for someone. You can give them your attention and listen well. When you're a giver, others will also give to you! It makes every day more fun.

THOUGHT OF THE DAY

What are some ways you can be a giver today?

PRAY TODAY

Dear God, thank You for giving me so many blessings. Help me be a giver too. Amen.

YOU BRING GOD JOY

"For the LORD your God is living among you. He is a mighty savior. He will take delight in you with gladness. With his love, he will calm all your fears. He will rejoice over you with joyful songs."

ZEPHANIAH 3:17 NLT

Do you know that you make God happy? The Bible says that God takes "delight in you with gladness" and that He "will rejoice over you with joyful songs." God loves watching over you and knowing what you're doing. He is excited when you learn new things, and your accomplishments bring Him joy. Because He is a loving Father, God celebrates when you do well. So whenever you are feeling small or unimportant, just remember that you are special and you bring great joy to God, your Savior!

THOUGHT OF THE DAY

You make God happy just by being YOU!

PRAY TODAY

Thank You, God, for loving me so much. I'm so glad that I can bring You joy! Amen.

CHOOSE TO BE GLAD

Every day is hard for those who suffer, but a happy heart is like a continual feast.

PROVERBS 15:15 NCV

I never get to be first." "You always get more than me." "I hate doing chores." Do you know someone who always complains? Complaining people often feel sad and angry. But did you know that complaining is a choice?

You can choose to change your thoughts from sad to glad. "This time I didn't get to be first, but maybe next time I will." "I don't have that toy, but I do have lots of fun things to play with." "I'm going to make a game of my chores today." You can choose to be glad! Try it!

THOUGHT OF THE DAY

When you feel like complaining or getting mad, choose instead a way to be glad!

PRAY TODAY

Dear God, thank You for loving me and giving me so much. Help me to choose to be glad for all my blessings. Amen.

KEEP ON GOING

But endurance must do its complete work, so that you may be mature and complete, lacking nothing.

JAMES 1:4 HCSB

If a runner decides to stop before getting to the finish line, she'll never win a race. If someone quits making a model car when they are only halfway finished, the car will never be complete. If you stop reading a book before you get to the end, you'll never know what happened. Our Bible verse today reminds us that it is important to endure (to keep on growing) if we want to become strong in our faith. Learning to follow Jesus takes time. Don't ever give up!

THOUGHT OF THE DAY

If you want to keep on growing, trust God to keep on going!

PRAY TODAY

Dear God, when it is hard to stay strong in my faith, will You please help me to never give up? Thank You for helping me to grow. Amen.

WHAT WILL HAPPEN NEXT?

"Do you think you can explain the mystery of God? Do you think you can diagram God Almighty? God is far higher than you can imagine, far deeper than you can comprehend."

JOB 11:7-8 MSG

The Bible tells us a lot about God. We know He loves and cares for everyone. We know He created everything in the universe. And we know He's great at surprises! God surprised Moses and the Israelites when He split the Red Sea. The disciples were very surprised (and a little scared!) when Jesus walked on water. And Jonah sure didn't expect that fish to swallow him whole! We don't know everything that will happen in the future, but we can trust that God will always care for us—in ways we may not expect!

THOUGHT OF THE DAY

Ask a grown-up how God has surprised them.

PRAY TODAY

Dear God, I can't wait to see how You surprise me! Thank You for always caring about me. Amen.

HELP YOUR FAMILY

The one who lives with integrity is righteous; his children who come after him will be happy.

PROVERBS 20:7 HCSB

Today's Bible verse says that when families live with "integrity," they are happy. Integrity means to be honest, to think of others first, and to do what is right. You can help your family to be happy by learning to making thoughtful choices. When you do something wrong, be honest and tell the truth. When you promise to do something for your parents, be sure you do it. Choose kindness! You will help your family be happy when you live with integrity!

THOUGHT OF THE DAY

How will you show integrity today?

PRAY TODAY

Dear God, thank You for giving me a family. Please help me to live with integrity so I can help us all be happy! Amen.

DAY 11

JUST ASK

If any of you lacks wisdom, you should ask God, who gives generously to all without finding fault, and it will be given to you.

JAMES 1:5 NIV

In school you learn to read, solve math problems, and understand how the world works. But you actually learn new things all the time—even when you're playing with your friends or spending time with family! And grown-ups are still learning too. Only God knows everything. So if you're ever wondering about anything—in school, with friends, or any time at all—ask God! He might help you figure it out on your own. He might lead you to a friend or grown-up who can guide you. But He always loves to help!

THOUGHT OF THE DAY

Don't be too shy to ask God why!

PRAY TODAY

Dear God, I have so many questions! Thank You for always listening and helping me. Amen.

TAKE GOOD CARE

So honor God with your bodies.

1 CORINTHIANS 6:20B NCV

God gave us each unique gifts so we can enjoy His world in our own special ways. But there's one gift God gave everyone: a body! And the Bible tells us that we can honor God by taking good care of this wonderful gift.

You help your body grow by eating healthy foods, getting enough sleep, and playing outside. You keep your body safe by wearing a seatbelt or a helmet. You use your body well when you help with chores, hug a friend, or pick up trash at the park. Your body is powerful. Use it well!

THOUGHT OF THE DAY

Can you think of three ways to help your body grow, keep it safe, and use it well?

PRAY TODAY

Dear God, thank You for my body! Help me take good care of it. Amen.

PARTY TIME

Celebrate God all day, every day.

PHILIPPIANS 4:4 MSG

There are certain days when we all celebrate God, like Christmas and Easter. But did you know that we don't have to wait for those special days? You can celebrate God any day you want to!

Why not throw God a party today? Make up a song about your favorite Bible story. Draw Him a picture of something you're thankful for or make a gift to share God's love with someone. Decorate your house with all the colors of the rainbow. Invite some friends over to join the fun! God is always worth a celebration—so make today a party day!

THOUGHT OF THE DAY

What would make a God party extra fun?

PRAY TODAY

Dear God, You are amazing! Help me celebrate You today and every day! Amen.

MORE FAITH

Immediately the father of the child cried out and said with tears, "Lord, I believe; help my unbelief!"

MARK 9:24 NKJV

Sometimes it is easy to have faith in God, but sometimes it's not. In today's verse, Jesus asks a worried father to believe that his sick son can be made completely well. The father has some faith, but he wants more. So, he asks Jesus for help. When you have a little faith, but you need more, you can ask Jesus for help too. Do you need more faith to try to learn something that is difficult? Do you need more faith to trust God to help you or your family? Ask Jesus. He wants to give you more faith.

THOUGHT OF THE DAY

When do you need more faith?

PRAY TODAY

Dear God, I have some faith, but sometimes I need more. Will You help me? Amen.

GOD'S SUPERPOWER

Finally, be strong in the Lord and in his mighty power.

EPHESIANS 6:10 NIV

Are there things that make you afraid? Maybe you're afraid of dogs, thunderstorms, the dark, or being asked to say something at school. When we know we can't control something, it can make us feel weak or fearful. God knows this, so He tells us we can count on His strength and mighty power instead of ourselves. God is more powerful than anything, and He wants to help us when we feel afraid. The next time you feel afraid, ask God to help you feel strong, and then count on His mighty power.

THOUGHT OF THE DAY

When will you count on God's strength?

PRAY TODAY

Dear God, thank You for Your mighty power. When I'm afraid, please help me count on You to be strong. Amen.

DAY 16

BE CONTENT

"You're blessed when you're content with just who you are—no more, no less."

MATTHEW 5:5 MSG

Jesus told His followers that the happiest people were those who learned to be content. To be content means you don't need more things to be happy—you like who you are and enjoy the things you have. Doesn't that sound great?

You might see other people and wish you were like them. Maybe they have more toys, or they are better at something you love to do, or they make friends more easily. Remember that God made you exactly right, and you don't need to change anything to earn His love. Trust the great plans He has for YOU!

THOUGHT OF THE DAY

Learn new things and make new friends, but never forget you matter because you are YOU.

PRAY TODAY

Dear God, when I compare myself to others, remind me that You love me for me! Amen.

DAY 17

THE GIFT OF GROWN-UPS

"Honor your father and mother. Then you will live a long, full life in the land the LORD your God is giving you."

EXODUS 20:12 NLT

Has God given you good grown-ups in your life? If so, thank Him for that! Parents, grandparents, aunts, uncles, or others who help and guide you each day are a wonderful gift. They share their wisdom and make good rules to keep you safe and healthy. They provide things you need like good food and a comfy home. And they worry about big (and sometimes boring) things so you don't have to! One of the best ways God cares for you is through the people who love you. So say thanks—to Him and them—today!

THOUGHT OF THE DAY

Your good grown-ups love you so. That's why they make rules, you know!

PRAY TODAY

Dear God, thank You for the people who love and guide me. Help me to honor and respect them today. Amen.

MAKE A CHOICE

"Choose this day whom you will serve. . . . But as for me and my house, we will serve the LORD."

JOSHUA 24:15 ESV

As a kid, you might feel like everyone makes decisions for you. But here's a secret—you always get to decide how you'll respond to what's happening! If your dad says it's time for bed, you can run and hide or you can get ready in time for a story. If your sister grabs your toy, you can yell at her or you can invite her to play together. If you notice someone is upset, you can ignore them or you can ask if they want a friend. We all make choices every day. Make sure yours reflect God's love!

THOUGHT OF THE DAY

What's a decision you might have to make today?

PRAY TODAY

Dear God, help me remember that I can always make the choice to honor You. Amen.

CREATE JOY

Do not neglect to do good and to share what you have, for such sacrifices are pleasing to God.

HEBREWS 13:16 ESV

Sometimes sharing feels like just giving something away. But did you know you actually create something too? You create joy—a lot of it!

When you share what you have, you bring joy to others. And because it feels good to make someone happy, that means you also bring joy to yourself. And the Bible says that God is pleased when we share what we have. So you've brought joy to God too! If all that joy can come from one moment of sharing, what might happen if you did it again and again? Why not give it a try?

THOUGHT OF THE DAY

With enough sharing, we can fill the world with joy!

PRAY TODAY

Dear God, it's not always easy to share what I have. Please help me do it more, so I can create joy all around! Amen.

GET THE ICKIES OUT

Tell your sins to each other. And pray for each other so you may be healed.

JAMES 5:16A NLV

Can you remember a time you made a mistake or a poor choice? Maybe you broke something or hurt someone's feelings. It can feel icky inside when that happens. You might want to pretend it didn't happen. But God has a different idea.

God asks us to tell each other when we've done something wrong. That's because something cool happens when you're brave enough to tell the truth: It gets the ickies out! Start by saying sorry, but don't stop there. Ask how to make things better and how to make safe, helpful choices next time! You'll be icky-less in no time!

THOUGHT OF THE DAY

If it's scary to share your mistakes, find a grown-up who can help you!

PRAY TODAY

Dear God, it's sometimes hard to tell the truth. Help me be brave, so I can send those icky feelings far away! Amen.

WHO DO YOU SEE?

Do you not know that you are the temple of God and that the Spirit of God dwells in you?

1 CORINTHIANS 3:16 NKJV

When you think about yourself, what do you see? Do you see the things you do well or the things that need work? Do you think about the last time you got in trouble or that funny joke you told? Do you like the person you're thinking about?

Here's what God sees: someone He loves very much. He will always rejoice in your happy times and help you through hard things. But He loves you exactly the way you are right now. You don't need to change anything to earn God's love; you already have it! So next time you look in the mirror, try to see what God sees: a beloved child!

THOUGHT OF THE DAY

Short or tall, brown eyes or blue, God loves what He sees in you!

PRAY TODAY

Dear God, thank You for loving me just the way I am! Help me love myself that way too. Amen.

PRAY FOR LEADERS

Pray for rulers and for all who have authority so that we can have quiet and peaceful lives full of worship and respect for God.

1 TIMOTHY 2:2 NCV

Who do you pray for? Most people pray for their friends or family. But did you know that leaders need your prayers too? Leaders can be well-known, like mayors or presidents, but they can also be people like teachers, doctors, pastors, or police officers. Leaders need to make decisions that affect others. They need wisdom about how to be fair and make sure others are cared for. That is a big responsibility, and they need God's help! Remember to pray for God to guide them so we can all lead peaceful lives.

THOUGHT OF THE DAY

Who are some leaders you can pray for?

PRAY TODAY

Dear God, thank You for giving us leaders. Please help them to make good decisions. Amen.

DAY 23

CHOOSE WISELY

Finally, brothers, whatever is true, whatever is honorable, whatever is just, whatever is pure, whatever is lovely, whatever is commendable, if there is any excellence, if there is anything worthy of praise, think about these things.

PHILIPPIANS 4:8 ESV

Every day you make many choices: Who will you play with? What will you watch? What will you read? What will you say? How will you spend your time? Our Bible verse reminds us that our choices are important. If we choose good things, we'll be happier and feel better. If we choose things that aren't so good, our minds and hearts will be filled with feelings that aren't so great—like fear and anger and unhappiness. You get to choose what you want to think about, so choose wisely.

THOUGHT OF THE DAY

What are some wise choices you can make today?

PRAY TODAY

Dear God, please help me to make wise choices. I want to fill my mind with good things. Amen.

LEARN AND HAVE FAITH

Yet faith comes from listening to this Good News—the Good News about Christ.

ROMANS 10:17 TLB

The Bible tells us that faith is being sure of something, even if you can't see it. At night, when it's dark, you know that the sun will rise in the morning—that's a kind of faith. And when you believe in God's love, that's faith too! You build faith in the sunrise by learning about the sun. You build faith in God by listening to the Good News of Jesus. Each time you hear stories about Jesus' love and the wonderful things He's done, you make your faith stronger. And a strong faith means God's love can shine bright in your heart!

THOUGHT OF THE DAY

What are some good things you know about Jesus?

PRAY TODAY

Dear God, I love to learn about Jesus. His love is forever—and that's very good news! Amen.

HELPFUL WISDOM

Listen carefully to wisdom; set your mind on understanding.

PROVERBS 2:2 NCV

Sometimes things feel too difficult. Maybe you're learning an instrument, or making friends at a new school, or there's a new baby at your house and things are just different. When you're having a tough time, try telling someone who's gone through the same thing. Ask your music teacher for new practice ideas. Talk to a friend who has a little sibling. And your parents have lots of experience making friends—ask how they do it! God has put wise people in your life. Listen to what they have to say!

THOUGHT OF THE DAY

People love to share their own stories. Never be afraid to ask for help!

PRAY TODAY

Dear God, when things get tough, please help me find—and listen to—wise people who can help. Amen.

GOD'S ALWAYS THERE

"Do not be afraid or discouraged. For the LORD your God is with you wherever you go."

JOSHUA 1:9B NLT

Try to think of a place where God isn't with you. You can't do it! The top of the tallest mountain? God is there. The bottom of the ocean? He's there too. Deep in the woods? In a super-crowded subway train? In your best hide-and-seek spot? Yep, yep, and absolutely! You can't hide from God, and you can't lose Him. He is never too busy to listen to your prayers. He runs every race with you, plays every game, dances every dance, and spends every moment by your side. So never fear—you're never alone!

THOUGHT OF THE DAY

God will never leave your side. You couldn't lose Him if you tried!

PRAY TODAY

Dear God, I'm so glad You're always with me, no matter where I go! Amen.

STOP AND PRAY

Don't worry about anything; instead, pray about everything. Tell God what you need, and thank him for all he has done.

PHILIPPIANS 4:6 NLT

What do you worry about? Some people worry a lot, and some worry a little, but the Bible says we can all do the same thing: pray.

When you pray, you tell God what you're worried about. He can handle all of it—whether there's a lot, a little, or somewhere in between. Praying reminds you that you're not alone, and God loves you. And when you add thanks to your prayer time, it's even better! Thanking God helps you remember all the good things He does and will continue to do. So next time you're worried, stop and pray!

THOUGHT OF THE DAY

Don't let worries ruin your day. Take a moment—stop and pray!

PRAY TODAY

Dear God, when I get worried, help me remember to pray and give You thanks. I love You! Amen.

DAY 28

PROTECTING ANGELS

For he will order his angels to protect you wherever you go.

PSALM 91:11 NLT

In the Bible, angels are often God's special protectors. When Daniel was thrown into the lions' den, an angel shut the lions' mouths so they would not harm Daniel. Another angel stood in the fiery furnace with Shadrach, Meshach, and Abednego, and they were not burned up!

You'll never end up in a den of lions or a giant furnace, but we all need God's help. Next time you feel afraid, lonely, or worried, ask God to send His angels to protect and comfort you. God loves to help His children, and He will never leave you alone.

THOUGHT OF THE DAY

You won't see God's angels with your eyes, but you might feel them with your heart.

PRAY TODAY

Dear God, thank You for the gift of angels. I'm never alone when I know You. Amen.

THE CHOICE IS YOURS

"Do everything the Lord your God requires. Live the way he wants you to. Obey his orders and commands."

1 KINGS 2:3A NIRV

Sometimes it can feel like the Bible is a book of rules. But actually, it's a book of choices. The shepherds chose to believe the angels at Christmas, and they got to meet Baby Jesus! Moses chose to challenge Pharaoh, and God used him to set the Hebrew people free. Jonah chose to ignore God's directions, and he got swallowed by a giant fish! (But then Jonah changed his mind, and the fish spat him out!) The Bible shows us that it's best to follow God's way, but He leaves the choices up to us. What will you choose?

THOUGHT OF THE DAY

What would it look like to choose God's way today?

PRAY TODAY

Dear God, I know Your way is best. Please help me make good choices, even when it's hard. Amen.

JOYFUL YOU!

Shout with joy to the LORD, all the earth! Worship the LORD with gladness. Come before him, singing with joy.

PSALM 100:1–2 NLT

Joy is one of God's great gifts. It's kind of like a deep, hopeful happiness mixed with love and thankfulness. When we trust God's good promises, we can feel joy no matter what's happening.

When people in the Bible felt joyful, they expressed it in lots of ways! Miriam played instruments. King David wrote songs and danced around. Nehemiah told people to throw a big party! When you feel joyful, you can sing, dance, paint pictures, help a friend, run around outside, or just say a prayer of thanks. There is no wrong way to feel joy!

THOUGHT OF THE DAY

Can you think of a time you felt joyful? What did you do?

PRAY TODAY

Dear God, thank You for the gift of joy! It reminds me You are always with me. Amen.

DAY 31

GOOD WORK!

So let's not get tired of doing what is good. At just the right time we will reap a harvest of blessing if we don't give up.

GALATIANS 6:9 NLT

"Good work!" Has anyone ever said that to you? Maybe you won a race or drew a cool picture. Maybe you told the truth, shared with a classmate, or stayed calm in a tough moment. Sometimes good work is something others can see. Other times, it's something no one can see. And a lot of times, good work is hard work. But the Bible tells us that doing good is always the right choice. So don't give up! Ask God to help you every day. He loves to tell you, "Good work!"

THOUGHT OF THE DAY

Can you think of some good work you've done?

PRAY TODAY

Dear God, I want to do good things, but it's not always easy. Will You please help me do good today? Amen.

GOD'S FOREVER LOVE

Surely goodness and mercy shall follow me all the days of my life, and I shall dwell in the house of the LORD forever.

PSALM 23:6 ESV

Some people think that if they try to follow God, nothing bad or sad will ever happen to them. But that is not what today's Bible verse means. It promises that God will always show His goodness and mercy to those who love Him. Even when hard times come along. Even when we get sick or hurt. Even when we feel lonely. God promises that He will always be with us, not only here in this life but forever! Nothing can take His love from us. God's love will never leave you! It lasts forever!

THOUGHT OF THE DAY

When has God shown His love to you?

PRAY TODAY

Dear God, I am so glad that Your love is forever. Help me to remember that You will never stop loving me! Amen.

GIVING THANKS

Praise the Lord. Give thanks to the Lord, for he is good; his love endures forever.

PSALM 106:1 NIV

When you love someone, you often want to do something kind for them or give them a gift. Did you know that because God loves you, He gives you good gifts too? God gives you family and friends, talents and skills, and a beautiful world to enjoy. He helps you when you're afraid, and He never leaves you. Actually, every good thing you enjoy is a loving gift from God! Our Bible verse today reminds us to give thanks to the Lord every day, to praise Him for His goodness, and to be grateful for all His good gifts.

THOUGHT OF THE DAY

What are three things you will thank God for today?

PRAY TODAY

Dear God, You are so loving. I am thankful for every good gift You have given me. Amen.

GOD'S PEACE AND JOY

"You will live in joy and peace."

ISAIAH 55:12A NLT

Happiness depends upon what happens to us—so we don't always feel happy. If someone gives us a present, we feel happy. If we don't get our way, we don't feel happy. But joy is something different. Joy is knowing that no matter what happens, God is always with us, and He loves us. Even when things don't go the way we want, we can still have joy. And that gives us peace deep in our hearts. When joy brings peace, little things don't bother us so much. Thank God for helping you feel joy, no matter what happens!

THOUGHT OF THE DAY

God wants to give His peace and joy to every single girl and boy!

PRAY TODAY

Dear God, I am so thankful that You help me to feel joy, no matter what happens! You are so good to me. Amen.

SERVE WITH A SMILE

Never be lazy, but work hard and serve the Lord enthusiastically.

ROMANS 12:11 NLT

God wants you to serve cheerfully and to be excited about the work you do! But how can you do that when you'd rather be doing anything else? Make it fun! Turn on some music and transform cleanup time into a dance party! Maybe you can sing a silly song to cheer up your brother. You could even pretend you DO feel like working! Tell yourself, "I just love setting the table! Forks are my favorite!" Get into a silly mood, and you'll serve with a smile every time!

THOUGHT OF THE DAY

Do you have chores? How can you make them fun?

PRAY TODAY

Dear God, I know You like it best when I serve with a smile. Please help me be happy to help others! Amen.

WHAT WILL YOU CHOOSE?

But Daniel made up his mind that he would not defile himself . . .

DANIEL 1:8A NASB

The Bible is full of stories about people who made choices. Some of them chose to do the right thing, and some chose to do the wrong thing. Daniel was a young man who chose to follow God's rules instead of obeying selfish King Darius. That made the king very angry, and he punished Daniel by throwing him into a pit filled with hungry lions. The king was sure the lions would eat Daniel. But God protected Daniel and shut the lions' mouths. Daniel made up his mind to follow God, and God took care of him!

THOUGHT OF THE DAY

When it's hard to choose the right thing to do, trust in God to take care of you!

PRAY TODAY

Dear God, please help me to be brave and choose to do what's right, even if it's hard or scary. Amen.

DAY 37

LET YOUR LIGHT SHINE

"You are the light of the world. A town built on a hill cannot be hidden. . . . Let your light shine before others, that they may see your good deeds and glorify your Father in heaven."

MATTHEW 5:14, 16B NIV

Jesus said that His followers are like light in a dark world. When you are kind, help others who need to be encouraged, or stand up for someone who is being mistreated, you are an example of His light of love and truth. People will see that you care about being a good friend. They see that your faith makes a difference. You can let your light shine or hide it. It is up to you!

The next time you see someone who needs help, give them a hand. Befriend someone who is lonely. Let your light shine.

THOUGHT OF THE DAY

Name some ways you can let your light shine today.

PRAY TODAY

Dear God, thank You for loving me. Help me to choose to let my light shine today so others can see how great You are. Amen.

GOD MATTERS MOST

"Do not have other gods besides Me."

EXODUS 20:3 HCSB

When God's people were trapped in Egypt, those around them worshipped lots of different gods. But when Moses led God's people out, God told them to worship only Him. God is real, and the other gods were not.

God didn't want His people to get distracted with things that weren't as important as following His loving ways. And He wants the same for you! It's wonderful to have big dreams and things you love to do. Just make sure that God is the most important thing of all. He has the best plans for you!

THOUGHT OF THE DAY

Nothing matters more than God.

PRAY TODAY

Dear God, I'm sorry I sometimes forget how awesome You are. Help me remember to always follow You! Amen.

OVERFLOW WITH HOPE

May the God of hope fill you with all joy and peace as you trust in him, so that you may overflow with hope by the power of the Holy Spirit.

ROMANS 15:13 NIV

If you carry a glass of milk that is full to the top, and someone bumps into you, what spills out? Milk! Whatever your glass is filled with overflows when you get bumped.

Do you know that you are like that full glass? If you are full of anger or fear and someone upsets you, those things overflow onto others. But if you trust Jesus to take care of you, God fills you up with joy, hope, and peace. Then, when life gives you some bumps, you will overflow with good things!

THOUGHT OF THE DAY

When you trust in God, you overflow with hope to everyone you know!

PRAY TODAY

Dear God, thank You that You want to fill my heart with joy and peace. Please help me put my trust in You so I can overflow with hope. Amen.

CHOOSE TO PRAY

Do not worry about anything, but pray and ask God for everything you need, always giving thanks.

PHILIPPIANS 4:6 NCV

When a thought pops into your head, you have a choice. You can worry about it or you can choose to pray about it. Did you meet a new friend, but you wonder if they want to play with you? Ask God to help you be friendly. At night, do you sometimes feel a little afraid when the light is off? Ask God to help you feel safe and cozy in your bed. Any time you talk to God, you are praying. He loves to hear and answer your prayers. Choosing to pray helps our worries go away!

THOUGHT OF THE DAY

What is something you can pray about today?

PRAY TODAY

Dear God, thanks for always hearing my prayers and helping me not to worry. Amen.

KEEP USING YOUR GIFTS

This is why I remind you to keep using the gift God gave you . . .

2 TIMOTHY 1:6A NCV

On your birthday or at Christmastime, you probably receive gifts from your parents. Parents give you gifts because they love you.

Did you know that God, our heavenly Father, also gives His children gifts? But they are not gifts that are bought at the store. God's gifts are special abilities or talents, and they are made just for you. You may be talented at art or music, or maybe you are good at helping people, listening, or teaching others how to do things. Keep using the gifts God gives you! You will be glad you did!

THOUGHT OF THE DAY

What are some of the gifts God has given you? How will you keep using them?

PRAY TODAY

Dear God, thank You for loving me and for giving me special gifts. Please help me to keep using them so I can be a blessing to others. Amen.

SLOW DOWN

To your knowledge, add self-control; and to your self-control, add patience.

2 PETER 1:6 NCV

What would happen if you were in such a hurry to eat your cookies that you only baked them half as long as the recipe said? Or how good would you be if you tried to play a baseball game after only swinging a bat one time? It takes time to do things the right way, to learn something new, or to get better at a skill. In the Bible, God reminds us that if we want to do something well, it is best to use self-control and be patient. When we slow down, we have time to learn, correct our mistakes, and get better!

THOUGHT OF THE DAY

Slowing down is sometimes the fastest way to do things well!

Dear Lord, thank You for reminding me to slow down. Please help me to be patient when I'm learning new things. Amen.

LISTEN BEFORE SPEAKING

My dear brothers and sisters, always be willing to listen and slow to speak.

JAMES 1:19A NCV

Have you ever said something you wish you could take back? Maybe you made a rude comment or called someone a name, and then you were sorry you spoke so quickly. Words are hard to take back once we have said them.

The Bible gives us some good advice in today's verse. Read the verse and see if you can find the advice. Being slow to speak means we take time to listen to what others say and then think carefully about our own words. Listening before speaking helps to save us from being sorry about what we say.

THOUGHT OF THE DAY

Can you think of a time when you spoke too soon? What happened?

PRAY TODAY

Dear God, please help me to listen before I speak. Let my words help others, not hurt them. Amen.

DAY 44

TRUST GOD

Commit everything you do to the LORD. Trust him, and he will help you.

PSALM 37:5 NLT

Trusting someone means you believe they will do what they say. The Bible says that when you ask God for help, you can believe that He will help you. Are you trying to learn something new? Trust God to help you! Do you need to stop a bad habit? Trust God to help you! Do you want to be more kind? God wants to help you do that too.

Don't forget that God loves you and cares about you. Ask for His help and then trust that He will do it!

THOUGHT OF THE DAY

What will you trust God to help you with today?

PRAY TODAY

Dear God, I am so glad I can always trust You to help me. Please remind me to ask for Your help today. Amen.

LEARN TO LAUGH

"He will yet fill your mouth with laughter, and your lips with shouting."

JOB 8:21 ESV

Larry loves jokes. Here are two of his favorites: "What vegetable earned all its merit badges? A Brussels Scout!" and "What did the Veggie say after a long day at work? I'm beet!"

Silly jokes and funny faces make us giggle and laugh. God wants us to enjoy life! And one way we can do that is to learn to laugh and be happy. Smiles are good for sharing, and making others happy is a great way to share joy with them. See if you can share some smiles today! You'll be glad you did!

THOUGHT OF THE DAY

What is your favorite joke? What makes you giggle?

PRAY TODAY

Dear God, thanks for helping me to be happy and joyful. Please help me to share smiles with others today. Amen.

YOUR SUPERPOWER

"This is my command—be strong and courageous! Do not be afraid or discouraged. For the LORD your God is with you wherever you go."

JOSHUA 1:9 NLT

Superheroes in books and movies often have a special power. Maybe they can fly, or they have a special cape, bracelet, or sword. It is easy to understand why they feel brave! But what about you? Are you sometimes afraid or worried, shy about speaking up or fearful of telling the truth? The Bible says you have the greatest superpower in the universe: "God is with you wherever you go!" When you believe this, you can be brave enough to do the right thing or conquer a hard job. With God, you are strong and courageous!

THOUGHT OF THE DAY

What will you be brave enough to do today?

PRAY TODAY

Dear God, I'm so glad that I can be brave because You are with me wherever I go. Amen.

BE WISE

Wisdom is more precious than rubies. Nothing you could want is equal to it.

PROVERBS 8:11 NCV

A great king named Solomon wrote this Bible verse. He was smart and strong. He had great armies and was very rich. But Solomon knew that none of that mattered if he did not have wisdom. Wisdom is knowing how to use what you have in ways that are right and good. If you have extra time or money, you can use it wisely to help others. If you have toys and books, you can use them wisely by inviting others to play and sharing with them. Ask God for wisdom to use what you have in the best possible way!

THOUGHT OF THE DAY

No matter your size, you can learn to be wise!

PRAY TODAY

Dear God, please help me be wise as I use what You have given me. Amen.

DAY 48

DO YOU WORRY?

Give all your worries and cares to God, for he cares about you.

1 PETER 5:7 NLT

When you worry about something it seems to get bigger! It's like filling a balloon with more and more air until it explodes! But God wants to help you.

You can tell Him about what worries you, and even try some ways to let go of your worries. Take some deep breaths and blow them out. Name three things you see, three things you hear, and then touch three different things to take your mind off your worries. Draw a picture of what you're worried about, then imagine giving it to Jesus! He cares for you!

THOUGHT OF THE DAY

What are some worries you will give to God?

PRAY TODAY

Dear God, please help me give my worries to You because I know You care about me. Amen.

DAY 49

BE A LOVING FRIEND

Finally, all of you should be of one mind. Sympathize with each other. Love each other as brothers and sisters. Be tenderhearted, and keep a humble attitude.

1 PETER 3:8 NLT

Today's verse has some great advice about being a good friend. Two important words are *sympathize* and *tenderhearted*. When you sympathize with someone, you listen well and show you care about their feelings. Being tenderhearted means that you are gentle and treat others with kindness. Imagine having a friend like that!

When you are tenderhearted and sympathize with others, friends know they can trust you to love them even when things are hard. They will see you are a caring friend, and they will want to be friendly with you too!

THOUGHT OF THE DAY

Who is a good friend to you? How will you be a good friend too?

PRAY TODAY

Dear God, please help me to be a good friend to others, to sympathize with them, and to be tenderhearted. Amen.

HIDDEN BLESSINGS

Every good and perfect gift is from above, coming down from the Father of the heavenly lights, who does not change like shifting shadows.

JAMES 1:17 NIV

People often think of blessings as all the good things they have. And it's true that God can bless us through wonderful friends and family, safe homes, silly pets, and sunny days. But God can also bless you through difficult things. That's because God's goodness never changes, even during hard times. If a friend moves away, perhaps God blesses you with His comfort and the chance to build new friendships. If you get hurt, God can bless you with the love and help of others. Every good thing comes from God, even those that are harder to see.

THOUGHT OF THE DAY

God's good work is never done. His blessings fall on everyone.

PRAY TODAY

Dear God, please help me find Your blessings in good times and bad! Amen.

THE PEACE JESUS GIVES

"Peace I leave with you; my peace I give you. I do not give to you as the world gives. Do not let your hearts be troubled and do not be afraid."

JOHN 14:27 NIV

When Jesus left His friends to return to heaven, He knew they would sometimes feel afraid and worried. So He gave them an amazing gift. He gave them His peace.

Jesus told them that His peace could calm their hearts and remove their fears. What a great gift! And do you know what is especially wonderful about that gift? He still gives it to us today! When you are afraid or nervous, worried or feeling shy, ask Jesus for His peace. He will help calm your fears and give you a heart filled with peace instead.

THOUGHT OF THE DAY

Can you think of some times when you might need the peace that Jesus gives?

PRAY TODAY

Dear God, I am so thankful that You promise to give me peace when I feel afraid or worried. Help me to remember to ask for the peace that Jesus gives. Amen.

STOP SPREADING ANGER

A gentle answer turns away anger, but a sharp word causes anger.

PROVERBS 15:1 NLV

When someone is mad, they often use angry words. Then the other person gets angry and shouts back. Pretty soon, everyone is upset and nothing has been solved! God knows that we all feel angry sometimes, but He wants us to keep that anger from spreading. How do we do that? Today's verse gives us a clue—use gentle words! It is hard to do, but practicing makes it easier. Try using gentle words like "I'm sorry," "I need some time to think," or "I can't talk about this right now," and you can turn away anger before it spreads.

THOUGHT OF THE DAY

Why should we stop anger from spreading?

PRAY TODAY

Dear God, when I'm angry, please help me to use gentle words instead of angry ones. Thank You. Amen.

KEEP GOD'S COMMANDS

This is how we are sure that we have come to know Him: by keeping His commands.

1 JOHN 2:3 HCSB

Do you know what a command is? It is an order or direction that tells you what to do or what not to do. Commands like "don't walk" and "stop" help keep us safe. Commands like "come in" and "keep out" tell us where to go. In the Bible there are special commands that help us know who God is and how He wants us to live. God says to "tell the truth," "give to those in need," "love one another," and "forgive." When we keep God's commands, we grow in faith and get to know Him better.

THOUGHT OF THE DAY

What is one of God's commands you can keep today?

PRAY TODAY

Dear God, thank You for giving me Your commands. Please help me to keep them so I can know You better. Amen.

LOOK FOR GOD

"But from there you will search for the LORD your God, and you will find Him when you seek Him with all your heart and all your soul."

DEUTERONOMY 4:29 HCSB

God does not hide from you. He promises that if you look for Him, you will find Him. But how do you look for God? Ask Him to show Himself to you: in the Bible, in other people, and in nature. Then be on the lookout for what is true, what is loving, and what is beautiful. God's truth can be found in the Bible. God's love can be found in the kindness of family and friends. And God's beauty can be seen in the world all around you. When you look for God, you will find Him!

THOUGHT OF THE DAY

Where will you look for God today?

PRAY TODAY

Thank You, God, for promising to always be with me. Help me look for You every day. Amen.

DAY 55

NEVER SEPARATED

And I am convinced that nothing can ever separate us from God's love. . . . No power in the sky above or in the earth below—indeed, nothing in all creation will ever be able to separate us from the love of God that is revealed in Christ Jesus our Lord.

ROMANS 8:38-39 NLT

If you have ever moved or had a friend move away, you know the lonely feeling of being separated from someone special. Maybe you had a pet that got lost or died. That's a lonely feeling too. Jesus makes a wonderful promise to us. He says He will never let us be separated from Him. His love is stronger than anything on earth or in the heavens. No matter where we go, how we feel, or what we do, we cannot be separated from God's love for us! He is always with us!

THOUGHT OF THE DAY

God's love is stronger than anything!

PRAY TODAY

Thank You that nothing can separate me from Your love, God. I'm so glad You are always with me. Amen.

CHANGE YOUR MIND

"Those who are pure in their thinking are happy. They will be with God."

MATTHEW 5:8 ICB

The Bible says we can choose how we think. If it rains on your birthday, you can choose to be mad or think of a way to enjoy your day anyway. If your friend gets sick and can't play, you can choose to stay grumpy all day or think about a way to help your friend feel better. When someone breaks your toy, you can choose to say mean words or to forgive them. With God's help, you can change your mind. This week try using your mind to think good thoughts at tough times. I wonder if you'll feel happier!

THOUGHT OF THE DAY

When you choose to think about how to make things better, you're thinking like God!

PRAY TODAY

Dear God, I want to think like You. Please help me learn to change my mind. Amen.

THERE'S ONLY ONE YOU!

"You're blessed when you're content with just who you are—no more, no less."

MATTHEW 5:5A MSG

Do you ever pretend to be someone different? Do you wish you were like one of your friends? Or maybe you wish you were a firefighter, or a princess, or a doctor, or a superhero!

It's fun to pretend, but it's also important to learn to be who God made you to be. There is only one you! Your ideas, talents, imagination, and body make up the special person God wants you to be. Don't ever forget that you are wonderfully made, and that God loves you. Remember to thank Him for making you YOU!

THOUGHT OF THE DAY

Name some things that make you special.

PRAY TODAY

Dear God, thank You for making me special. Help me to be the best "me" I can be! Amen.

THE GOLDEN RULE

"Just as you want others to do for you, do the same for them."

LUKE 6:31 HCSB

One day Jesus gave His friends some important advice: Think about how you want to be treated, then be sure to treat others that way too. Today we call this advice the "Golden Rule."

The Golden Rule is an easy way to remember how to be a good friend. Do you like when people help you? Then be sure to help others. Does it feel good when others forgive you? Share that feeling by being forgiving as well! Obey the Golden Rule and you will be living as Jesus wants you to.

THOUGHT OF THE DAY

What is one way you can follow the Golden Rule today?

PRAY TODAY

Dear God, thank You for teaching me how to live. Please help me to follow the Golden Rule today. Amen.

GOD'S FAMILY

"And I will be a father to you, and you shall be sons and daughters to me, says the Lord Almighty."

2 CORINTHIANS 6:18 ESV

Families come in all shapes and sizes. They are big or small, noisy or quiet, rambunctious or calm, or some combination of all those things! God loves all families and even calls us His sons and daughters. He is our loving parent, and He wants us to remember to treat others as if they were our brothers and sisters. That means we love them and take care of them. We look for ways to help out and have fun together. God welcomes all kinds of people into His family, because there's always enough room for everyone!

THOUGHT OF THE DAY

What are some interesting things about your family?

PRAY TODAY

Dear God, thank You for loving me and inviting me to be in Your family. I'm so glad You are my loving Father. Amen.

YOU CAN BE SURE

For the LORD will be your confidence, And will keep your foot from being caught.

PROVERBS 3:26 NKJV

This verse talks about "confidence." That's a word that means being sure of something. If you learn to kick a ball, ride a scooter, or sing a song, you become confident you can do it well. But there are other things you might not feel so sure about—like how you will do at school, whether someone will be your friend, or what will happen tomorrow. Today's Bible verse reminds us that God will be our confidence in any situation. Any time you aren't sure about something, remember that you can be sure that God is always with you!

THOUGHT OF THE DAY

What's something you aren't sure about? How will you trust God for help?

PRAY TODAY

Dear God, thank You that You are always with me. Please help me put my confidence in You. Amen.

THE GIFT OF PEACE

"I promise to be with you and keep you safe, so don't be afraid."

JEREMIAH 1:8 CEV

When Jesus left His disciples and returned to heaven, He gave them a gift. He gave them His peace. Then He said, "I do not give to you as the world gives." What did that mean? In the world, things always wear out, disappear, or even die. But when Jesus gives us something, it lasts forever. Jesus wanted His friends to know that they could always have His peace in their hearts. When you feel worried or upset, you can count on Jesus to give you His peace too. Ask Him for His never-ending gift. It's yours!

THOUGHT OF THE DAY

When was a time you needed Jesus' gift of peace?

PRAY TODAY

Dear Jesus, thank You for giving me the gift of peace. Help me to count on You when I feel worried or afraid. Amen.

PRAISE GOD

"Praise the name of God forever and ever, for he has all wisdom and power."

DANIEL 2:20 NLT

The Bible says it's important to praise God. That's because praising God reminds us that He can do anything and that He loves each and every person. We praise God when we tell Him we know how great He is. We also praise Him when we thank Him for being loving, wise, and powerful. You can sing songs to Him, pray, raise your hands in worship, or sit quietly and think about how wonderful He is. And you can praise Him anytime, anywhere! So why not spend some time in praise today?

THOUGHT OF THE DAY

What is something you can praise God about right now?

PRAY TODAY

Dear God, I'm glad You are so powerful, wise, and kind. Thank You for loving me. Amen.

BIG AND SMALL

"Remembering the words the Lord Jesus himself said: 'It is more blessed to give than to receive.'"

ACTS 20:35B NIV

How do you feel when you help people? Do you feel happy when you work hard to make a special gift for your grandma or cheer loudly for a friend? Doing good things can feel great! Sometimes it may seem like your small decisions don't matter. Does anyone care that you're keeping your promises each day, or not sharing gossip, or sitting with a friend who feels left out? Yes! God cares! You make the world better with every good choice, and God is so proud of you. Keep choosing good actions, big and small. Everything you do matters!

THOUGHT OF THE DAY

Doing good is a big deal—even when it's something small!

PRAY TODAY

Dear God, sometimes I forget to make good choices in the small things. Help me do good things of every size, every day! Amen.

THE "GREEN-EYED MONSTER"

Don't set your heart on anything that is your neighbor's.

EXODUS 20:17B MSG

Have you ever wanted what someone else has? Let's say your friend has a cool new bike. Suddenly, you don't like your bike anymore. You want your friend's bike instead. Soon, all you can think about is the bike that you don't have. Wanting what someone else has is called envy. Some people call envy "a green-eyed monster"! It's a monster because it gobbles up all your joy and can even ruin friendships. But you can destroy this icky beast! Start thanking God for what you have. List all the blessings you can think of! The "green-eyed monster" of envy will run away from a heart filled with thankfulness.

THOUGHT OF THE DAY

Name five things you're thankful for.

PRAY TODAY

Dear God, I'm so thankful for every blessing I have. Please help me to remember my blessings when I envy others. Amen.

STRONG AND WONDERFUL

The LORD *your God is God of all gods and Lord of all lords. He is the great God, who is strong and wonderful.*

DEUTERONOMY 10:17A NCV

When Moses wrote the book of Deuteronomy for the people of Israel, he told them many important things. But the most important was that their God was different than any of the other gods or lords that the people around them worshipped. He wanted them to know that their God was the one true God, who was more powerful than anything *and* loved them more than they could imagine. He wanted them to know that God was both strong and wonderful. And because God never changes, you can trust that He is still strong and wonderful today, and His love will never go away.

THOUGHT OF THE DAY

What are some wonderful things you know about God?

PRAY TODAY

Dear God, thank You for being strong and wonderful. Help me to always trust in You. Amen.

FOLLOW THE DIRECTIONS

Now if you really obey the LORD . . . God will set you high above all nations on earth.

DEUTERONOMY 28:1 CEB

Larry was so excited about his new construction set! But nothing was working out. He got more and more frustrated. When Bob came by, Larry showed him the messed-up project.

"Did you follow these?" asked Bob, holding up the directions. He sat down with Larry and they carefully followed each step. Soon the project was finished, and it looked great!

God gives us directions in the Bible too! When we ignore them and do things our own way, we often end up disappointed! But when we obey what God says, things always work out better.

THOUGHT OF THE DAY

When we obey, God shows us the way!

PRAY TODAY

Dear God, please help me to obey You so that I can learn the right way to live. Amen.

IRON SHARPENS IRON

As iron sharpens iron, so people can improve each other.

PROVERBS 27:17 NCV

Our verse today uses picture language. It talks about how someone might rub a dull knife blade against another piece of metal to make the blade sharp again. Then, the verse reminds us that people working together, helping, guiding, and teaching can improve each other too. Have you ever helped someone learn how to do something? Has someone helped you? Maybe they showed you how to ride a bike or skateboard, to play a song on the piano, or to do a craft project. When people work together to learn or teach something, they both get sharper! It's like iron sharpening iron!

THOUGHT OF THE DAY

How has someone helped you to improve?

PRAY TODAY

Dear God, thank You for giving me friends and family who help me learn and grow. Amen.

DON'T GIVE UP

Don't burn out; keep yourselves fueled and aflame. Be alert servants of the Master, cheerfully expectant. Don't quit in hard times; pray all the harder.

ROMANS 12:11-12A MSG

Have you ever wanted to learn to do something that was difficult? Maybe you're trying to learn to read, or hit a baseball, or ride a bike, or do a trick on a skateboard. You try and try, but you keep making mistakes. When that happens, it is easy to give up and just quit. God knows how hard you are working, and He wants you to stay hopeful and not give up. Ask Him to help you when you feel discouraged. Pray and trust, then keep on working. God will help you!

THOUGHT OF THE DAY

Where do you need God's help to keep from giving up?

PRAY TODAY

Dear God, thank You for hearing my prayers when I feel like giving up. Help me to keep on trying. Amen.

WORK AT GETTING ALONG

Work at getting along with each other and with God.

HEBREWS 12:14 MSG

God made each person, but He didn't make us all the same. Some of us are loud and some are quiet. Some people love sports and others love to read. Some people enjoy being with groups and others like to be alone. We all have different ideas too. Our differences make us special and interesting! But sometimes differences can make us feel frustrated with each other. God understands, but He wants us to get along, even when we disagree. When you meet someone with ideas different from yours, don't get angry—get curious! Ask questions. Try to understand them. Be friendly. Work hard to get along!

THOUGHT OF THE DAY

When you meet someone different from you, how can you work at getting along?

PRAY TODAY

Dear God, please help me to be accepting of all kinds of people. Amen.

GOD'S GOOD RULES

This is love for God: to keep his commands.

1 JOHN 5:3 NIV

Some people think that rules just ruin our fun. But what if there were no rules? Drivers would go any speed they wanted, and no one would stop to let people cross the street. People would show up for school or work whenever they felt like it. Robbers could steal whatever they wanted! Rules actually help us and make life safer! That's why God gives His people good commands (or rules) to follow. Rules like: be kind, tell the truth, and help others. He knows that when we love Him enough to follow His good rules, we can live safe and happy lives.

THOUGHT OF THE DAY

Can you name some of God's good rules that you will follow today?

PRAY TODAY

Dear God, thank You for protecting me by giving me good rules. Please help me to obey them. Amen.

DAY 71

CHOOSING WHAT'S RIGHT

"Do what is right and true. Be kind and merciful to each other."

ZECHARIAH 7:9B NCV

Every day you have many different choices to make. How will you answer when your mom or dad asks you to help out? Will you share with your friend? Will you admit when you make a mistake? Will you say "sorry" to someone if you hurt their feelings? The Bible says that doing what is right and true means choosing kindness and mercy. If you sometimes have a hard time deciding what to do, remember today's verse. Ask yourself, "What is the kind thing to do?" Then choose to do that!

THOUGHT OF THE DAY

When was a time you chose the right thing to do? How did it feel?

PRAY TODAY

Dear God, I want to make good choices. Please help me choose to be kind and merciful to others today. Amen.

BE A GOOD FRIEND

A friend loves you all the time.

PROVERBS 17:17A ICB

Good friends are there when you're happy and when you're sad. They understand when you are having a hard day. They listen to your ideas and help you solve problems. It's great to have good friends.

But it's just as important to BE a good friend. When your friend has something hard to do, are you willing to help out? When your friend wins a game or gets something special, are you happy for them? Remember that friendship goes both ways. If you want to have good friends, you need to be a good friend.

THOUGHT OF THE DAY

How can you be a good friend today?

PRAY TODAY

Dear God, thanks for my good friends. Please help me to be a good friend today. Amen.

TALKING TO GOD

"But when you pray, go into your private room, shut your door, and pray to your Father who is in secret."

MATTHEW 6:6A HCSB

Sometimes families pray together before meals or at bedtime. But God, your loving Father, also wants you to take time to talk with Him all by yourself. What does He want to hear about? Well, just like when you're talking to a good friend, you can talk to God about anything at all! Tell Him what you're glad about. Explain to Him why you feel worried or afraid. Let Him know how thankful you are for your blessings. And be sure to ask Him to help you as well as the people you care about. Talking to God every day helps you feel closer to Him!

THOUGHT OF THE DAY

What will you talk to God about today?

PRAY TODAY

Dear God, thanks for always being ready to listen to me. Please help me make time to talk with You today. Amen.

PUT ON YOUR BELT

Stand firm then, with the belt of truth buckled around your waist.

EPHESIANS 6:14A NIV

Did you know that there's something besides your clothes that you should put on every day? The Bible calls it "the belt of truth." That's a word picture describing how God's truth surrounds us and protects us just like a Roman soldier's sword belt.

Jesus said, "I am the Truth!" and Scriptures say that God's Word is true. So we can put on the "belt of truth" every day by following Jesus and memorizing verses from the Bible. Here are some great ones: "All things are possible with God" (Mark 10:27 NIV) and "I am with you always" (Matthew 28:20 NIV). Wear your belt all day!

THOUGHT OF THE DAY

Can you remember a Bible verse that helps you?

PRAY TODAY

Dear God, thank You for giving me a belt of truth. Help me remember to put it on every day. Amen.

GROWING GOOD FRUIT

But the fruit of the Spirit is love, joy, peace, patience, kindness, goodness, faithfulness, gentleness, self-control; against such things there is no law.

GALATIANS 5:22-23 ESV

When you see apples and bananas in the grocery store, you know they didn't grow there. They grew where someone took care to plant and water them. The Bible uses picture language to say that God's Spirit wants to grow good fruit in your life. But the fruit of God's Spirit isn't apples or bananas! Read today's verse again. What kinds of fruit does God want to grow in you? When you read your Bible, pray, and obey God, you're helping God's Spirit to water and grow this kind of good "fruit" in you!

THOUGHT OF THE DAY

What will you do to help God grow good fruit in you?

PRAY TODAY

Dear God, thank You for giving me Your Spirit. Please help me to grow good fruit for You. Amen.

IMPORTANT DIFFERENCES

Always be humble, gentle, and patient, accepting each other in love.

EPHESIANS 4:2 NCV

There are many different kinds of people in the world. Old and young, active and quiet, bold and shy—we're not all the same! God has created us with differences, and that's what makes life interesting . . . and sometimes hard.

Because we have different ideas, we don't always agree. That means we need to listen to one another, be patient, and try to learn from each other. You might have a great idea, but someone else might too! The Bible says we should accept others and then work together, showing love to each other.

THOUGHT OF THE DAY

Why do you think God made us different from each other?

PRAY TODAY

Dear God, thank You for creating us with differences. Please help me to listen to others and work together with them in loving ways. Amen.

FOLLOW GOD'S EXAMPLE

Follow God's example, therefore, as dearly loved children.

EPHESIANS 5:1 NIV

Have you ever tried on your dad's or mom's shoes and walked around in them? Do you ever help one of your parents make cookies or wash the car? Maybe you've even tried to copy the way a parent talks! Following a parent or copying the way they do things is an important way that children learn and grow.

The Bible says we should follow God's example too. God cares for people—do you? God helps and encourages His children. Are you also a helper and an encourager? When you follow God's example, you will become more like Him!

THOUGHT OF THE DAY

What is one way you can follow God's example today?

PRAY TODAY

Dear God, thank You for making me Your child. Please help me to follow Your example today. Amen.

WHAT IS THE BIBLE?

Every part of Scripture is God-breathed and useful one way or another.

2 TIMOTHY 3:16A MSG

You might think of the Bible as one big book, but it is actually a library of sixty-six books! These books were written over hundreds of years by dozens of different writers. They contain laws, history, poetry, prophecy, and stories. But each part of the Bible tells us important things—about God and about how He wants us to live. We can learn from every part of the Bible. When you read the Bible, ask yourself some questions: Who are the people in this story? What can I learn from this? How does this help me live as God wants?

THOUGHT OF THE DAY

What is something you have learned from the Bible?

PRAY TODAY

Dear God, thank You for the Bible. Please help me learn about how You want me to live as I read it. Amen.

GOD REALLY SEES YOU

"God does not see the same way people see. People look at the outside of a person, but the LORD looks at the heart."

1 SAMUEL 16:7B NCV

When we look at others, what do we notice first? Their skin color, hair color, or maybe the clothes they're wearing? Guess what? When God looks at people, He doesn't care about those things! He looks at what kind of person they are. Are they kind? Do they care about others? Do they have big dreams? Are they afraid or upset? God loves each of us enough to know what is in our hearts. He cares about how we feel and what we think. You can always be sure that God really sees you and that He loves you very much.

THOUGHT OF THE DAY

Here's good news that's really true: God sees you and loves you too!

PRAY TODAY

Dear God, I'm so glad You really see me and know me. Thank You for loving me so much. Amen.

DAY 80

BE GENTLE

Always be gentle with others. The Lord will soon be here.

PHILIPPIANS 4:5 CEV

When you hold a little chick or pet a kitten, you need to use gentle hands so you don't hurt them. When you talk to a baby, you need to use a gentle voice so you don't scare her. But gentleness is important with others too. If you push or pinch someone, you might hurt them. If you yell at them or call them names, you might hurt their feelings. God wants us to be good friends. He says we should always be gentle with others. Each person you know is special to God, so treat others with gentleness!

THOUGHT OF THE DAY

Who is gentle with you? Who will you treat gently today?

PRAY TODAY

Dear God, I'm so glad You are gentle with me. Please help me to be gentle with others too. Amen.

YOU CAN ALWAYS COME BACK

Come back to the LORD your God, because he is kind and shows mercy. He doesn't become angry quickly, and he has great love.

JOEL 2:13B NCV

In the Bible, God tells us how to love and care for ourselves and others. When we choose to do what God says, it's like moving even closer to Him. When we don't do what He says, that's called sin. And every time we sin, it's as if we move away from God. But guess what? We can always come back.

You come back to God when you tell Him what you did and ask for forgiveness. When you ask, He will forgive you right away! He'll never stop loving you, and He's always ready to welcome you back.

THOUGHT OF THE DAY

God never stops loving you and me.

PRAY TODAY

Dear God, I'm sorry for the times I sinned. Please forgive me, and bring me close to You again! Amen.

SHOWING LOVE

Love is patient and kind, never jealous, boastful, proud, or rude. Love isn't selfish or quick tempered. It doesn't keep a record of wrongs that others do.

1 CORINTHIANS 13:4-5 CEV

The Bible says that Jesus loves us and that we should love one another. But what does love look like? The apostle Paul wrote a letter to believers to explain what love is. It says: When you are patient, you are showing love. When you don't insist on having your own way or always being first, you are showing love. When you don't get mad over every little thing, you are showing love. When you forgive someone, that's love. These are just a few of the ways you can show love to others! How will you show love today?

THOUGHT OF THE DAY

Showing love is the best way to follow Jesus every day!

PRAY TODAY

Dear God, thank You for showing love to me. Please help me show love to others. Amen.

GOD PAYS ATTENTION

But God did listen! He paid attention to my prayer. Praise God, who did not ignore my prayer or withdraw his unfailing love from me.

PSALM 66:19–20 NLT

Do you know that God always hears your prayers? He listens when you tell Him how you're feeling. He is glad when you thank Him, when you praise Him for who He is, and when you sing songs to Him. When you ask for things in your prayers, He always answers. Sometimes His answer is "yes," sometimes it is "no," and sometimes it is "wait." Because He knows you and loves you, you can trust that His answer is good, and He will help you handle whatever comes along. God pays attention to your prayers because He loves you and cares for you!

THOUGHT OF THE DAY

What will you say to God today?

PRAY TODAY

Dear God, thank You for always paying attention to my prayers. Help me to trust You and talk to You each day. Amen.

STAY OUT OF IT

Any fool can start arguments; the honorable thing is to stay out of them.

PROVERBS 20:3 GNT

When you're angry, it's easy to lose your temper, yell, and even fight! But while that might be an easy choice, the Bible warns that it's also a foolish one. Fighting can hurt people, and angry arguments can damage friendships. God says it's better to stay away from both.

So, try actually staying away! Take a break in your room, walk to the other side of the playground, or just do something different. When you feel calmer, you can try again. Chances are, the other person will feel better too, and you can find a solution everyone is happy with.

THOUGHT OF THE DAY

Where is a safe place you can go when you're angry?

PRAY TODAY

Dear God, I know fighting is the wrong choice. Help me make a safe choice when I get angry. Amen.

REAL HAPPINESS

Be happy with what you have. God has said, "I will never leave you or let you be alone."

HEBREWS 13:5B NLV

What makes you happy? Maybe your friends, family, or pets? Or winning your favorite game, eating a special treat, or just playing with your favorite toys? Every good thing you have is a gift from God, and of course those things make you feel happy! But there's a special happiness that doesn't depend on what you have or who you know. God says He will never leave you or let you be alone. He knows you, loves you, and will always guide you. Things and people can make you feel happy for a while, but knowing God loves you can make you happy forever! That's real happiness!

THOUGHT OF THE DAY

How does knowing God loves you make you happy?

PRAY TODAY

Dear God, I'm so happy that You are always with me! Thank You for loving me so much. Amen.

GOD'S WILL

Rejoice always! Pray constantly. Give thanks in everything, for this is God's will for you in Christ Jesus.

1 THESSALONIANS 5:16-18 HCSB

Have you ever heard someone talk about "God's will"? It means something that God wants. And the Bible actually tells us exactly what God's will is for YOU! He wants you to rejoice, pray, and be thankful every day. Why? Rejoicing and prayer help you feel closer to God, so you can have His peace, joy, and comfort whenever you need them (and share them with others). And practicing thankfulness is one of the best ways to notice and enjoy all His good gifts. God's will is for you to live your very best life!

THOUGHT OF THE DAY

Whenever you pray, start with praise and thanks!

PRAY TODAY

Dear God, thank You for Your good will for my life! Help me rejoice, pray, and say thanks every day. Amen.

GOD'S PERFECT TIME

He has made everything beautiful in its time.

ECCLESIASTES 3:11A NIV

Because God created everything, He knows the perfect time for everything. He knows when the sun should rise, when flowers should bloom, and when fruit should ripen. He knows the right time for babies to be born. He knows just the right way for you to grow and learn too. You may want to grow faster or master a skill more quickly. But God knows the perfect time for everything. Keep trying, learning, and practicing, then trust Him to make everything beautiful at just the right time!

THOUGHT OF THE DAY

God knows the perfect time for everything!

PRAY TODAY

Dear God, I'm so glad You know the right time for everything in my life! Help me trust You more each day. Amen.

WHAT DO YOU NEED?

And my God will supply every need of yours according to his riches in glory in Christ Jesus.

PHILIPPIANS 4:19 ESV

God promises to supply everything we need. That doesn't mean gifts will come raining down from the sky! Instead, God provides in ways that are just right for you. Are you having trouble in school? Maybe God has put another student in your class who can help—all you have to do is ask! Is it hard to fall asleep at night? God's comfort is just a prayer away! Ask God to show you the ways He's already given you what you need. Then trust Him to keep caring for you just as He has promised.

THOUGHT OF THE DAY

Did you know that love is a basic need? Who has God given you to love?

PRAY TODAY

Dear God, I'll bet I don't even notice all the gifts You have given me! Thank You for providing exactly what I need. Amen.

DAY 89

REAL FORGIVENESS

You will throw away all our sins into the deepest part of the sea.

MICAH 7:19B NCV

Sometimes when we've done something wrong and ask for forgiveness, the other person says they will forgive us, but then they keep reminding us of our mistakes. And that makes us feel bad all over again.

God never does that. When we ask God to forgive us, He not only forgives us, but He also gets rid of our sins. The Bible says He throws all those forgiven sins into the deepest part of the ocean! He never reminds us of our mistakes, and He loves to give us another chance. God's forgiveness is for real and forever!

THOUGHT OF THE DAY

When you ask God to forgive you, He always does!

PRAY TODAY

Dear God, thank You for giving me real forgiveness that lasts forever. Amen.

NO HIDE-AND-SEEK

"God did this so that [people] would seek him and perhaps reach out for him and find him, though he is not far from any one of us."

ACTS 17:27 NIV

Have you ever played hide-and-seek? It's a fun game to play with friends, but do you know who won't ever play hide-and-seek with you? God! God wants everyone to find Him, so He never hides from us. He is always near, and we can talk to Him anytime or anywhere. You can talk to God at school or home, on the playground, or in your bed at night. You never have to guess where God is. He loves you so much that He always stays close to you.

THOUGHT OF THE DAY

God will never hide from you.

PRAY TODAY

Dear God, thank You for always staying close to me. I'm so glad You love me. Amen.

DAY 91

A BETTER WAY

For if you refuse to act kindly, you can hardly expect to be treated kindly. Kind mercy wins over harsh judgment every time.

JAMES 2:12-13B MSG

The Bible says we shouldn't be surprised if we do something mean and then someone is mean to us too. Name-calling leads to more name-calling. Hitting leads to more hitting. But the Bible also tells us about a better way. If we are kind even when someone else is mean, we can help stop the meanness and change it to something better. When you are kind, even if it's hard, you are making a choice to follow the example of Jesus. When you refuse to be mean, you are showing others a better way.

THOUGHT OF THE DAY

When unkind words are easy to say, just stop and choose a better way!

PRAY TODAY

Dear God, please help me to choose kind words when I'm tempted to say something mean. Amen.

GOD ALWAYS HEARS YOU

Be gracious to me, Lord, for I call to You all day long.

PSALM 86:3 HCSB

Do you talk to God before you eat? Do you say prayers at bedtime? Maybe you pray when you're at church or Sunday school. The Bible reminds us that anytime is a great time to talk to God. God is never on vacation or asleep or too busy to listen to you. He loves hearing from you any time of the day or night. And there isn't just one way to pray either! You can sing to God, whisper to Him, tell Him about your day, or ask Him questions. He's always happy to hear from you!

THOUGHT OF THE DAY

What's your favorite time to talk to God?

PRAY TODAY

Dear God, I'm glad You're always there to hear me. Thanks for loving me so much. Amen.

GOD IS WITH US

"For where two or three are gathered together in My name, I am there among them."

MATTHEW 18:20 HCSB

God lives in the heart of each person who loves Him. That's why He says that whenever we get together with others who love Him, He is with us! It doesn't matter if you are old or young or if there are hundreds of people or just two or three—whenever God's people gather, He is there. He hears your singing and praying. He is there when you read the Bible together and when you care for one another. Remember that whenever you are with others who love and believe in God, He's right there with you!

THOUGHT OF THE DAY

Give thanks to God for being with His people!

PRAY TODAY

Dear God, I'm so glad that You live in me and that You are with Your children whenever we get together. Amen.

CHOOSE TO TRUST

Those who know Your name will put their trust in You. For You, O Lord, have never left alone those who look for You.

PSALM 9:10 NLV

Do you know what it means to trust in God? It means to choose to believe what God says about Himself. In the Bible, God says that He loves you. He says that He will never leave you. He says He will help you. He says He will always forgive you. Because God is trustworthy, you can count on Him to do exactly what He says. Sometimes you may not feel like God is there, but trusting God is a choice, not just a feeling. Choose to trust God and He will never let you down.

THOUGHT OF THE DAY

Is it ever hard to trust God?

PRAY TODAY

Dear God, I love You and I'm so glad You love me too. Please help me to choose to trust You every day. Amen.

FAITH MAKES THINGS POSSIBLE

Jesus replied, "Why do you say 'if you can'? Anything is possible for someone who has faith!"

MARK 9:23 CEV

"Faith" is a Bible word that means believing and trusting that what God says is true. If you believe what Jesus says, you can do anything. You can forgive someone who hurt your feelings because Jesus says forgiving helps both of you. You can share with someone because Jesus says it's important to help others. You can obey your parents because God tells you that's the right choice. You can tell the truth because that's what God wants you to do. All these things are hard, but they are all possible when you have faith.

THOUGHT OF THE DAY

What's something you can do because you have faith in God?

PRAY TODAY

Dear God, please help my faith grow so that I can do anything You want me to! Amen.

GOD'S BETTER WAY

A man's heart plans his way, but the LORD determines his steps.

PROVERBS 16:9 HCSB

Sometimes we have great ideas, but God's plans are different. That's hard to understand when it happens. Maybe you were really hoping to join the soccer team, but there was no room, so you have to do something else instead. That's disappointing! But if you keep a good attitude, you might find that the new thing is even better! You could meet a great new friend or discover something new you love to do. When your plans don't work out, it's OK to feel upset. But remember to ask God what He's planning. Maybe He's guiding your steps in a better way!

THOUGHT OF THE DAY

Make good plans for every day but pray for God to lead the way!

PRAY TODAY

Dear God, thank You for leading me every day. Please help me keep a good attitude and follow Your way. Amen.

WORDS AND ACTIONS

Faith by itself isn't enough. Unless it produces good deeds, it is dead and useless.

JAMES 2:17 NLT

How do you know you can trust or believe someone? Do you listen to what they say, or do you watch what they do? If their actions don't match their words, watch out!

If someone says they are a follower of Jesus, they should act the way Jesus says to act. They should be kind. They should help others. They should be honest. Your actions show others if your faith is true or not. Ask yourself this: *If someone couldn't hear a single word I said, would they know I follow Jesus because of my actions?* Make sure the answer is yes!

THOUGHT OF THE DAY

Help me show my faith is true, by what I say AND what I do!

PRAY TODAY

Dear God, thank You for loving me. Please help me to act in ways that show others I trust in You! Amen.

LEARNING TO TRUST

"The LORD who saved me from a lion and a bear will save me from this Philistine."

1 SAMUEL 17:37A NCV

When David was young, he spent years caring for his family's sheep. David trusted God to protect him and to help him be brave. Sometimes David had to fight off lions and bears with just a sling and stones! David learned that when he trusted God, God always helped him.

Then one day, David faced a different kind of enemy: a Philistine giant named Goliath. Because David had learned to trust God when he fought lions and bears, he knew he could also trust God to help him fight Goliath. And he was right! God helped David defeat the giant.

THOUGHT OF THE DAY

Can you think of some times when you needed to learn to trust God?

PRAY TODAY

Dear God, I'm so glad You are always with me. Please help me to learn to trust in You. Amen.

USE WORDS CAREFULLY

LORD, help me control my tongue; help me be careful about what I say.

PSALM 141:3 NCV

Can you guess how many words a person speaks in a day? Hundreds? Thousands? Scientists say that we each say between 6,000 and 15,000 words in a day. That's a lot of words! And the Bible says to be careful about the ones we choose to say.

Words can help, but they can also hurt. Can you remember a time when someone's words made you feel better? What about a time when words hurt your feelings or made you sad? Ask God to help you use your words carefully. Be a helper, not a hurter!

THOUGHT OF THE DAY

What are some helpful words you can speak today?

PRAY TODAY

Dear God, will You help me to be careful with my words today? I want to help others, not hurt them. Amen.

ARE YOU HUMBLE?

Always be humble and gentle. Be patient and accept each other with love.

EPHESIANS 4:2 ICB

Some people think that if they are humble, it means they are weak. But the truth is that being humble shows a super strong faith!

A humble person knows they don't have to brag or be first. They don't need to put someone else down to feel good about themselves. A humble person trusts that God will take care of them. They enjoy putting others first, giving compliments, listening, forgiving, and accepting others who are different from them. God says that being humble is a way to show love.

THOUGHT OF THE DAY

Being humble is a way to love each other every day!

PRAY TODAY

Dear God, sometimes it is hard to be humble. Will You please help me to put others first today? Amen.

FAITH, HOPE, AND LOVE

There are three things that remain—faith, hope, and love—and the greatest of these is love.

1 CORINTHIANS 13:13 TLB

The Bible says that there are three things that are very important. They are faith, hope, and love. Faith means trusting in God and what He has done for you. Hope means believing that God will do what He has promised. And love means acting in ways that show you have both faith and hope in God! Do you treat others with kindness? Are you patient and forgiving when things don't go your way? When you have faith and hope in God, it is easier to show love to others because you know God always takes care of you!

THOUGHT OF THE DAY

Name three ways you can show love to your family and friends today.

PRAY TODAY

Dear God, I am so glad I can always trust You to take care of me. Please help me to be loving to others today. Amen.

TRUTH TAKES STRENGTH FROM GOD

We say they are happy because they did not give up.

JAMES 5:11A NCV

It's amazing to see star athletes, musicians, and artists do what they do. But they weren't always that way—everybody starts as beginners! They worked hard to get so good, and most of them still work hard to stay that way.

Beginning something can be hard . . . and sometimes boring. But if you want to get better at anything, you can't give up! God can help. When you feel frustrated, ask God for strength to try again. If you get bored, ask God to help you find fun in each step. When you don't give up, you get better every day!

THOUGHT OF THE DAY

God is always with you, so you'll always have help!

PRAY TODAY

Dear God, thank You for helping me when things get hard. Help me never to give up on things that matter! Amen.

PRACTICE

We are part of the same body. Stop lying and start telling each other the truth.

EPHESIANS 4:25 CEV

Is it ever hard to tell the truth? You're not alone! Even people in the Bible had trouble with lying sometimes. But God says that being honest is always the best choice—even when we don't feel like it.

So how do you get better at doing something hard? Just practice! Tell the truth about small things, so you'll be ready when big things come along. And if you've already told a lie? It's not too late! Tell the person what happened and see if you can help make things right. As you practice more and more, the truth will become much easier than lying!

THOUGHT OF THE DAY

Practice telling the truth until it becomes a habit.

PRAY TODAY

Dear God, sometimes it's so hard to tell the truth. Will You please help me practice whenever I can? Amen.

BETTER THAN ONE

Two people are better off than one, for they can help each other succeed. If one person falls, the other can reach out and help. But someone who falls alone is in real trouble.

ECCLESIASTES 4:9-10 NLT

Even if you're someone who likes to do things by yourself, sometimes it's nice to spend time with other people. Stuck on an art project? A friend can help you think up new ideas! Bored of playing by yourself? Invite your younger sibling to play with you! And do you ever have feelings that are confusing? Sharing them with a parent or a teacher you trust can help you work through a problem or at least feel a little better. God has put people in your life to build you up and help you grow!

THOUGHT OF THE DAY

Who is someone you like spending time with?

PRAY TODAY

Dear God, please help me enjoy my alone time and work well with others too! Amen.

DO YOU LOOK LIKE GOD?

So God created human beings in his own image.

GENESIS 1:27A NLT

Have you ever noticed that some people look alike? Brothers and sisters sometimes look similar; good friends might even dress the same after a while!

God made each of us in His image—that means we all look a little like Him on the inside. How cool is that?! Each of us can imagine how others feel and choose to put their needs above our own. We can create and imagine new things. We can love and be loved. And each time we choose to do these things, others will see God in us a little more clearly.

THOUGHT OF THE DAY

Who do you think you look like? What's a way you can "look" more like God?

PRAY TODAY

Dear God, I'm so proud to be in Your family. Help me look more like You each day. Amen.

DAY 106

USE KIND WORDS

A kind answer soothes angry feelings, but harsh words stir them up.

PROVERBS 15:1 CEV

We all get angry. Maybe our feelings were hurt, or someone pushed ahead of us in line. Maybe we wanted to have something and our parents said no. You can't help feeling angry, but you can help what you say when you're mad or upset.

If we use angry words, we just make things worse. It's like stirring up a fire. But if we use kind words and don't yell or scream, it calms down the angry feelings. It isn't easy, but things go so much better if we remember to use kind words instead of angry ones.

THOUGHT OF THE DAY

Choose some kind words you can say next time you're feeling upset. It helps to have a plan!

PRAY TODAY

Dear God, please help me to use kind words instead of mean ones when I feel angry. Amen.

DOING THINGS THE RIGHT WAY

All things should be done in the right way, one after the other.

1 CORINTHIANS 14:40 NLV

Whether you want to build a model plane or make some pancakes, you need to do things the right way. If you just take a bunch of plastic pieces and glue them together, it probably won't look like an airplane. Or if you just dump flour and milk and eggs together, you might get a bowl of gooey glop instead of a yummy breakfast. Because God loves us, He gives us directions in the Bible like "be kind" and "love one another." When we follow God's directions, we do things the right way, and they usually turn out well!

THOUGHT OF THE DAY

Doing things the right way means listening and following God each day.

PRAY TODAY

Dear God, thank You for giving me good directions in the Bible. Please help me follow You and do things the right way. Amen.

GOD'S ON YOUR SIDE

Now the God of all grace, who called you to His eternal glory in Christ Jesus, will personally restore, establish, strengthen, and support you . . .

1 PETER 5:10 HCSB

Do you ever feel frustrated? Or just lonely or confused? There's Someone special who is always cheering you on. Whether you are feeling sad or glad or even if you're feeling mad, God is right beside you. He loves you and wants to help you, no matter what's going on. Nothing worries God and nothing is too hard for Him.

Next time you feel like you need a little help, talk to God about it. He's on your side and He wants to help you. He will give you strength to do hard things and patience to get through tough times.

THOUGHT OF THE DAY

With God on your side, you can face anything!

PRAY TODAY

Dear God, thanks for always being on my side. Please help me to remember to talk to You whenever I need help. Amen.

SHOW GOD'S LOVE

We know how much God loves us, and we have put our trust in his love. God is love and all who live in love live in God, and God lives in them.

1 JOHN 4:16 NLT

If you love God, He lives in you. But how will anyone else know that? Because God is love, you can show He's living in you by letting His love shine through you in what you do and say. When you help someone, share what you have, or speak up for someone who is being teased, you are showing that God lives in you. Any time you say kind, helpful words instead of mean, hurtful words, you are letting God's love shine through you. People may not be able to see God, but they can see God's love when you share it with others!

THOUGHT OF THE DAY

Pick two ways you will show God's love today.

PRAY TODAY

Dear God, I'm so glad You love me. Help me look for ways to show Your love to others today. Amen.

PRACTICE PATIENCE

But they that wait upon the L*ORD shall renew their strength; they shall mount up with wings as eagles; they shall run, and not be weary; and they shall walk, and not faint.*

ISAIAH 40:31 KJV

Do you hate to wait? It's sometimes hard to be patient! Maybe you feel frustrated when the things you want to do seem too hard right now. God understands, and He gives you a wonderful promise. He says that if you will be patient, then at just the right time, He will help you do the things He created you to do. And even better, He will give you the strength to do them well! Trust that God is there to help you and be patient. You and God will do amazing things!

THOUGHT OF THE DAY

What is something you need to be patient about?

PRAY TODAY

Thank You, God, for helping me to grow. Please help me be patient as I wait for Your help. Amen.

LOVE IN ACTION

Love is patient, love is kind.

1 CORINTHIANS 13:4A HCSB

Some people think that love is just a feeling. But God says that love is much more than a feeling. Love is an action. It is something you do. Our verse tells us two ways that we can act with love. We can be patient—we can wait without complaining, take turns, and let others go first. And we can be kind—we can listen, share, and help. When we act with love, we show others that love is more than just a feeling. Love is something you do!

THOUGHT OF THE DAY

What are some ways you can put your love into action today?

PRAY TODAY

Dear God, thank You for being patient and kind. Please help me put love into action today. Amen.

YOUR BODY, GOD'S TEMPLE

Don't you know that you are God's temple and that God's Spirit lives in you?

1 CORINTHIANS 3:16 NCV

There are many things that make you special, but one of the most amazing is that God says you are His temple. A temple is the place where God lives. In Old Testament times, the temple was a building in Israel. But after Jesus returned to heaven, He sent His Spirit to live in each person who believes in Him. That makes your body God's temple! When you take care of your body you honor God. Eating good food, exercising, making safe choices, and getting enough rest are all good ways to take care of God's temple!

THOUGHT OF THE DAY

What are some ways you take care of your body?

PRAY TODAY

Thank You, God, for giving me such an amazing body. Help me to honor You by taking good care of it. Amen.

AN OVERFLOWING LIFE

"I came that they may have and enjoy life, and have it in abundance [to the full, till it overflows]."

JOHN 10:10B AMP

If you hold a cup under running water, it fills up and then, when it is full, the water overflows. It splashes out of the cup and runs all over the place! That's a picture of how Jesus wants you to be. He wants to fill you up with His love and joy so much that they overflow and splash all over everyone you know! So when you love others, are kind to them, and help them to find joy, you are doing exactly that—you're overflowing with what He has given to you!

THOUGHT OF THE DAY

Learn to let love overflow to every person that you know!

PRAY TODAY

Dear Jesus, please help me to overflow with Your love and joy as I play with my friends today. Amen.

FEELINGS

There is a right time for everything: . . . A time to cry; A time to laugh; A time to grieve; A time to dance.

ECCLESIASTES 3:1, 4 TLB

Everyone has feelings. You might feel happy one day and sad the next. Sometimes you feel like dancing and other times you feel like being quiet. God created us with the ability to feel different ways at different times. The Bible reminds us it's OK to have these feelings. And if our feelings ever seem too big to keep inside, we can talk to a parent or a friend. We can tell God about it too! It's good to share your feelings and to understand that no matter how you feel, God's love for you never changes.

THOUGHT OF THE DAY

God always loves you . . . no matter how you feel!

PRAY TODAY

Dear God, I'm glad You care about my feelings. Help me to remember that You love me all the time! Amen.

CHOOSE TO TRUST GOD

When I am afraid, I will trust in You.

PSALM 56:3 HCSB

Did you know that everyone feels afraid sometimes? Even teenagers and grown-ups feel afraid. Some of us are afraid of getting lost, or being alone, or not doing well in a game or at school. The world is a big place and there is so much we don't know. That's why the Bible reminds us to trust in God whenever we feel afraid. God made the world, and He created you too! He is greater than anything we fear. When we choose to trust in Him, He will calm our hearts and help us be less afraid.

THOUGHT OF THE DAY

Give your fears to God. He is big enough to take care of them!

PRAY TODAY

Dear God, I'm so glad You are greater than my fears! Help me to trust in You all the time! Amen.

DOING HARD THINGS

"I say to you who are listening to me, love your enemies. Do good to those who hate you. Ask God to bless those who say bad things to you. Pray for those who are cruel to you."

LUKE 6:27-28 ICB

When Jesus taught people how to live, He sometimes asked them to do hard things. In our verse today, Jesus tells His friends to be kind and loving to people who are mean and hateful. That isn't easy. But Jesus knows that love is more powerful than hate, and kindness is greater than meanness. When we pray for and try to love those who treat us poorly, we are showing them God's way to live. And if we will do the hard things He asks us to do, Jesus can use us to shine His love in the world and even change people's lives!

THOUGHT OF THE DAY

How will you show love to someone today?

PRAY TODAY

Dear God, I want to do the hard things You ask me to do. Please help me to be kind and loving today. Amen.

SPEND TIME TOGETHER

Therefore encourage and *comfort one another and build up one another, just as you are doing.*

1 THESSALONIANS 5:11 AMP

The people in your family probably enjoy different things. That's great, because God gave each of us unique gifts! But it's not great when it leads to arguments over how to spend your time.

So what can you do? Take turns being the chooser! Let your brother choose the family board game, then you can choose the bedtime story. Try your dad's favorite pizza shop, even if you were hoping for tacos. And maybe you don't enjoy your cousin's baseball game, but isn't it fun when she comes to your dance recital? Being a family means the best time is time spent together.

THOUGHT OF THE DAY

How does your family spend time together?

PRAY TODAY

Dear God, I love my family. Help us all share what we love with each other! Amen.

ASK FOR HELP

Remember what you are taught. And listen carefully to words of knowledge.

PROVERBS 23:12 ICB

Do you ever have trouble remembering how to do something? Maybe you're figuring out a new game, trying to play a new instrument, or learning something tough at school. It's easy to get confused and frustrated when you're trying to cram new information into your brain!

It can be helpful to try slowing down. Take breaks. Practice the simpler steps over and over until you're super comfortable with them before moving on. And don't be afraid to ask for help. God has given you good friends, parents, coaches, and teachers who have lots of knowledge to share. You don't have to do it alone!

THOUGHT OF THE DAY

Everyone struggles to learn something new. That's why God gave good teachers to you!

PRAY TODAY

Dear God, I get so frustrated sometimes! Please show me how to slow down, listen, and ask for help. Amen.

SHARE GOD'S LOVE

"This is how everyone will recognize that you are my disciples—when they see the love you have for each other."

JOHN 13:35 MSG

There's a story in the Bible about a man who liked to brag about giving offerings and praying. He was very proud of himself and wanted everyone to know that he was following God and doing everything right. But Jesus says that's the wrong way to do it! If you want to show that you love Jesus, then all you need to do is love people. Be a friend to someone who is lonely. Help a younger sibling (or an older one!). Share a hug when a friend is sad. When you care for others, God's love shines through.

THOUGHT OF THE DAY

Loving Jesus means sharing His love with others.

PRAY TODAY

Dear God, I want everyone to know how much I love You. Help me show people Your love every day! Amen.

RESPECT BRINGS RICHES

Being respected is more important than having great riches.

PROVERBS 22:1A ICB

When you respect someone that means you care about how they feel. You listen to what they have to say. You help them when they have a problem. You take time to be with them. Respect is a gift you give to another person. It doesn't cost any money, but the Bible says respect is better than riches! Respecting someone tells that person you think they are important. When someone shows you respect, you feel special too! And when you give respect to others, they will often respect you back. Then you both feel richer!

THOUGHT OF THE DAY

Name some ways you will show a friend you respect them today.

PRAY TODAY

Dear God, please help me to be a person who gives the riches of respect to others. Amen.

BE THANKFUL?

We can rejoice, too, when we run into problems and trials, for we know that they are good for us—they help us learn to be patient. And patience develops strength of character in us and helps us trust God more each time we use it until finally our hope and faith are strong and steady.

ROMANS 5:3-4 TLB

How do you feel when you make a mistake? Embarrassed? Frustrated? How about . . . excited?

Does that sound crazy? The Bible says we should actually be thankful for mistakes and hard times. Those are perfect times to practice beautiful things like patience, humility, and hope. Patience because we may have to work diligently to fix something. Humility because we might need to ask for help or forgiveness. And hope because we need to trust that God will make things right. These things build our faith and friendship with God. If we were perfect, we wouldn't get to do any of that!

THOUGHT OF THE DAY

Can you think of a mistake you've made? What did you learn from it?

PRAY TODAY

Dear God, thank You that even mistakes can be beautiful when You're with me! Amen.

BE A LIGHT-BRINGER

Walk as children of light (for the fruit of light is found in all that is good and right and true).

EPHESIANS 5:8B-9 ESV

What does it mean to "walk as children of light"? Does it mean to wear shoes that glow in the dark? Does it mean to carry a flashlight around all the time? No! When the Bible says "walk as children of light," it means we should try to live in ways that please Jesus. Be kind. Say words that help people, not hurt them. Tell the truth. If someone does something that makes you mad, try to forgive. Speak up when you see something unfair. These kinds of things shine the light of Jesus into the world. So be a light-bringer wherever you go!

THOUGHT OF THE DAY

Can you sing "This Little Light of Mine"?

PRAY TODAY

Dear God, thank You for shining Your light on me. Help me to be a light-bringer everywhere I go today. Amen.

GOD ALWAYS FORGIVES

Those who hide their sins won't succeed, but those who confess and give them up will receive mercy.

PROVERBS 28:13 CEB

Have you ever done something wrong and then tried to cover it up? Maybe you told a lie, or you blamed someone else. But when you do that, you probably still feel afraid and worried that someone might find out. God says that when we do something wrong, we need to say we did it and ask to be forgiven. God loves to forgive His children. He wants you to learn from your mistakes and try again. You never have to be afraid to tell God what you've done wrong. He will always forgive you.

THOUGHT OF THE DAY

God loves to forgive His children.

PRAY TODAY

Dear God, I'm sorry for the times I've done things that were wrong. Thank You for loving and forgiving me. Amen.

SMALL BECOMES GREAT

"There's a youngster here with five barley loaves and a couple of fish! But what good is that with all this mob?"

JOHN 6:9B TLB

Once Jesus was teaching and a great crowd of people were listening. At dinnertime they were hungry, but they had no food. Then a boy gave Jesus his small lunch. Jesus prayed and a great miracle happened: Suddenly there was enough food for everyone! Because the boy shared, everyone was blessed. You can share what you have too. Even if you think it is something small, Jesus can use it to do great things! You can share your time, your help, your smiles, your snacks, or your toys. It may seem small, but Jesus can make it great!

THOUGHT OF THE DAY

What will you share today?

PRAY TODAY

Thank You, God, for Your many blessings. Please help me share what I have so You can use it to bless others. Amen.

GOD WILL HELP YOU

Commit everything you do to the LORD. Trust him, and he will help you.

PSALM 37:5 NLT

When you need to do something that is hard or scary, how do you feel? Do you worry? Do you whine? Do you get mad and refuse to do it? Going to a new class, visiting the dentist, staying overnight at Grandma's house, and going on a trip are all things that might seem hard. But God says He will help you if you trust Him. You can tell Him about your feelings and He will give you courage, calm your fears, and help you do hard things. God always loves to help you. All you have to do is ask!

THOUGHT OF THE DAY

When was a time God helped you do something hard?

PRAY TODAY

Dear God, I'm so glad You are always ready to help me. Thank You for loving me so much. Amen.

A LITTLE FAITH

"Truly I tell you, if you have faith as small as a mustard seed, you can say to this mountain, 'Move from here to there,' and it will move. Nothing will be impossible for you."

MATTHEW 17:20B NIV

Sometimes people think that bigger means better. You can buy supersized sodas and giant packs of cereal or cookies. There's even a place where you can buy a beach ball as tall as your ceiling! But did you know that the Bible says you only need a small bit of faith to do amazing things? It's true. Do you know why? It's because your faith is in our great God. When you trust and believe in Him, you are counting on God's power, not your own. And God can do all things. He is bigger—and better—than anything!

THOUGHT OF THE DAY

Small faith + a great God = miracles!

PRAY TODAY

I'm so glad that You are such a great God! Thank You for taking my small faith and doing wonderful things! Amen.

CHOOSE WHAT'S GOOD

I can do anything I want to if Christ has not said no, but some of these things aren't good for me.

1 CORINTHIANS 6:12A TLB

You make choices every day. Some choices are between what's right and wrong. But other choices are about what's good for you. You need to sleep, but it isn't good for you to stay in bed all day. It's important to eat, but not so great to eat only cookies. It's fine to have toys, but it's not good to beg and whine to get more and more toys. A wise person learns to choose what is good. The next time you make a choice, remember to ask God if it is a good choice.

THOUGHT OF THE DAY

What is a good choice you can make today?

PRAY TODAY

Thank You, God, for what You've given me. Help me to always choose what is good for me. Amen.

DAY 128

CLIMB INTO JOY

A cheerful heart does good like medicine.

PROVERBS 17:22A TLB

Feeling grumpy is no fun. Some people call it being "down in the dumps." But building a cheerful heart makes it easier to climb out of those dumpy, grumpy feelings!

So how do you get a cheerful heart? Every day, find something to be happy about. It can be something small like a pretty flower, or something big like a birthday party. When you build the good habit of seeing God's blessings all around you, your heart will get used to being cheerful. Then on grumpy days, your cheerful heart will boost you out of the dumps!

THOUGHT OF THE DAY

What made you feel cheerful today?

PRAY TODAY

Dear God, thank You for Your wonderful world. Please help me find reasons to be cheerful each day! Amen.

GOD'S GIFT TO YOU

This is the day that the LORD has made; let us rejoice and be glad in it.

PSALM 118:24 ESV

Do you know that God gives you a gift every day? What about today? What will happen? Who will you see? Beginning a fresh new day is a little like opening a present! So why not start the day by thanking God for it? Tell Him how glad you are for everything He has given you: a body so you can enjoy the world, a mind so you can think and dream, the rain and sunshine, plants and animals, friends and family. Every new day comes from God, and He wants you to enjoy it!

THOUGHT OF THE DAY

At the start of each new day, give thanks to God, rejoice, and pray!

PRAY TODAY

Thank You, God, for making this day. I'm so glad You love me and want me to be filled with joy! Amen.

GOD'S CURE FOR SIN

But if we confess our sins to God, he can always be trusted to forgive us and take our sins away.

1 JOHN 1:9 CEV

Sin is when we do things our way instead of God's way. Everyone in the world sins because we all want things our own way. But sin doesn't make us happy for very long, and it doesn't make God happy either. That's because sin pulls us away from God and from other people too.

Since God loves us, He wants us to be close to Him. God says that if we will tell Him about our sins and ask Him to forgive us, He will! When God takes our sins away, we feel close to God again and closer to others too.

THOUGHT OF THE DAY

Telling God about our sin lets God's forgiveness come right in!

PRAY TODAY

Dear God, thank You for Your loving forgiveness that cures my sin. Help me to live like You want me to. Amen.

JESUS LOVES YOU NO MATTER WHAT

But God showed how much he loved us by having Christ die for us, even though we were sinful.

ROMANS 5:8 CEV

Do you think you have to do everything right? Are you afraid of trying something new because you might make a mistake? The Bible says that Jesus loves you no matter what. So you can be brave! You can try new things without worrying about making mistakes, because you can never lose God's love.

Jesus loves you so much that He gave up His life so you could live with Him forever. He knows you and He cares for you—even when you make mistakes. He wants to help you and He will never leave you.

THOUGHT OF THE DAY

How does Jesus' love help you to be brave?

PRAY TODAY

Dear God, thank You for loving me so much. Please help me to trust in Your love every day. Amen.

WHAT DOES PATIENCE LOOK LIKE?

Let your patience show itself perfectly in what you do. Then you will be perfect and complete and will have everything you need.

JAMES 1:4 NCV

The Bible says to be patient, but does that mean we just sit around and wait for things? Not quite! Patience also means trusting that something good is coming—and knowing that it can't be rushed.

So HOW can you be patient? If you're waiting, try to wait without complaining. If you want to get better at something, work slowly and don't skip anything. If you're trying something new, don't give up if it doesn't work at first. Show your patience by being calm, hardworking, and brave. Then, God can help you do amazing things!

THOUGHT OF THE DAY

What will your patience look like today?

PRAY TODAY

Dear God, it's hard to be patient. Please help me to trust that You have good plans for me. Amen.

LEARNING FROM MISTAKES

"Forget what happened before, and do not think about the past. Look at the new thing I am going to do."

ISAIAH 43:18B-19A NCV

It doesn't feel good to make a mistake. We want to get everything right the first time. But did you know that mistakes are important too? They help us learn to do better next time!

When you make a mistake, whether you trip on the soccer field, smear a painting, or say something mean, try these three steps. First, say to yourself, "I'm OK—no one is perfect!" Second, make things right or get help if you need to. And third, decide what you'll try differently next time. Then stop worrying! Your mistakes don't bother God. He loves to help you try again.

THOUGHT OF THE DAY

Ask a grown-up about a time they learned from their mistakes.

PRAY TODAY

Dear God, I'm glad I don't have to be perfect! Please help me learn from my mistakes so I can grow each day. Amen.

REMEMBER TO TELL THE TRUTH

Don't ever forget kindness and truth. Wear them like a necklace. Write them on your heart as if on a tablet.

PROVERBS 3:3 NCV

Sometimes it is hard to tell the truth. Maybe you did something you knew was wrong, and you were afraid you would get in trouble. Maybe you don't want to tell the truth because someone might make fun of you. But telling the truth is so important that God says to "wear the truth like a necklace" and "write truth on your heart." Those are word pictures that mean we should be honest wherever we go. Give it a try. When you practice telling the truth, it becomes easier and easier to do.

THOUGHT OF THE DAY

Practice telling the truth today in everything you do and say!

PRAY TODAY

Dear God, thank You for Your words of truth in the Bible. Help me be a person who remembers to tell the truth. Amen.

WORDS THAT LIFT

Be gracious in your speech. The goal is to bring out the best in others in a conversation, not put them down, not cut them out.

COLOSSIANS 4:6 MSG

Who do you talk to each day? Your parents and siblings? Teachers and friends? New kids you meet? We all do a lot of talking, so it's important to think about the words we use. Some words lift people up and make them feel good—like thanking someone for their help or sharing what you like about them. Other words can hurt people, like teasing, yelling, or even refusing to say anything at all! God wants us to think carefully about our words, so that we always help people feel better. Look for kind words you can say to and about others today.

THOUGHT OF THE DAY

Can you think of a time someone's words lifted you up?

PRAY TODAY

Dear God, I'm so thankful that You always lift me up. Help me to use my words to lift someone else up today. Amen.

PAY ATTENTION!

"If you have ears, pay attention!"

MATTHEW 11:15 CEV

Do your parents ever remind you to pay attention? Jesus said the same thing to His disciples and followers! We all get distracted sometimes—but if we don't pay attention, we can miss important things.

When someone is talking, try to look at their eyes. That will help you focus on their words too. If you're listening to a Bible story, think of one question you will ask about it afterward. And when you pray, it can help to write down what you want to say. Paying attention is the best way to learn, grow, and have fun!

THOUGHT OF THE DAY

Notice what people say, but also how they say it. That will help you be a better friend!

PRAY TODAY

Dear God, please help me focus when I get distracted. I don't want to miss anything! Amen.

FIND JOY IN GOD

But let all those rejoice who put their trust in You; Let them ever shout for joy, because You defend them; Let those also who love Your name be joyful in You.

PSALM 5:11 NKJV

When you're having a bad day, it's not always easy to feel better. But the Bible tells us that no matter what, we always have a reason to be joyful: God is on our side!

That doesn't mean you won't ever feel sad or angry. It just means that you have a Friend who can help. Every time you think about something that's bugging you, try to make your next thought about God. You could say thanks for something good, ask for help, or just tell Him how you feel. God is always there for you. And that's something to be happy about!

THOUGHT OF THE DAY

Why does God want us to be joyful?

PRAY TODAY

Dear God, thank You that You're always there to help me. Help me to remember You when I'm feeling down. Amen.

HE'S GOT THE POWER!

I pray . . . that you may know . . . his incomparably great power for us who believe.

EPHESIANS 1:18-19A NIV

Have you ever tried to turn on a lamp or a nightlight when it's not plugged in? Nothing happens! But once you plug it in again, it shines as bright as ever. All it needed was power!

God is our source of power. When we're not connected to Him, we start to forget what we're designed to do. We might get stuck in frustrations that keep us from enjoying His beautiful gifts! When you start to feel that way, try plugging back into God. Pick up your Bible, hum a song from church, or say a simple prayer. God's power is waiting for you!

THOUGHT OF THE DAY

Stay powered up by starting each day with a Bible verse!

PRAY TODAY

Dear God, when I feel far from You, please remind me to plug back into Your awesome power! Amen.

ASK AND GROW

. . . so that you will live the kind of life that honors and pleases the Lord in every way. You will produce fruit in every good work and grow in the knowledge of God.

COLOSSIANS 1:10 NCV

Do you have a lot of questions about God? That's great! The Bible says we can always learn something new about His wonderful ways.

You can learn from Bible stories and listening to teachers and pastors. God can also help you find answers when you pray. As you spend more time with God, you might realize you want to know even more! So keep asking questions—God gave you a curious mind that can wonder and imagine. Don't be afraid to use it!

THOUGHT OF THE DAY

Even grown-ups are still learning. See if you can work together to discover something new!

PRAY TODAY

Dear God, I hope I always want to know more about You! Thank You for my curious mind. Amen.

PRAISE ALWAYS!

My mouth is filled with your praise, and with your glory all the day.

PSALM 71:8 ESV

What do you love most about God? He is a Friend who will never leave us. He created a beautiful world, full of trees and stars and animals and laughter! He made your mind to be like no one else's, with unique ideas and plans. His gifts of friends and family help make you who you are. He knows your every thought, and He loves you more than you could imagine. There are so many reasons to praise God. Pick one, and try to thank Him during your day. Then tomorrow, pick another one! When you spend your days praising God, you'll never run out of reasons to.

THOUGHT OF THE DAY

Fill your days with thanks and praise!

PRAY TODAY

Dear God, Your world is amazing, and everything You make is good. I love You! Amen.

WHAT MAKES A FRIEND?

Every time I think of you, I give thanks to my God.

PHILIPPIANS 1:3 NLT

How do you feel when you think about your friends? Are you excited to play with them? Do you laugh, thinking about a funny joke you shared? Or maybe you just feel thankful! A good friend listens to your ideas, enjoys spending time with you, and encourages you to be yourself. Friends should make us feel good about who we are.

If a friendship makes you feel nervous, scared, angry, or sad, that's not OK. And it's definitely not what God wants for you! Ask Him to help you find friends you can be thankful for.

THOUGHT OF THE DAY

What do you think makes someone a good friend?

PRAY TODAY

Dear God, thank You for the gift of friendship. Please help me find, and be, a very good friend! Amen.

DAY 142

TRY BEING KIND

And we know that for those who love God all things work together for good, for those who are called according to his purpose.

ROMANS 8:28 ESV

Have you ever felt nervous about doing something kind? Maybe you want to take cookies to your new neighbor, but you feel shy. Or you notice someone being left out. You suspect they'd like to play, but what if they say no? God promises that He can make good come from any situation, especially when we're following Him. Usually, folks will be grateful for your kindness. But even if you don't get the response you wanted, trust that God is still doing good work with your good deeds. And next time you feel the nudge to be kind, try again!

THOUGHT OF THE DAY

A kind choice is a good choice.

PRAY TODAY

Dear God, when I feel shy, help me remember that You are with me. We can be kind together! Amen.

HE KNOWS HOW YOU FEEL

For God called you to do good, even if it means suffering, just as Christ suffered for you. He is your example, and you must follow in his steps.

1 PETER 2:21 NLT

Do you ever wish you could hear God's voice? In a way, you hear it every day! When you know the right thing to do, that's God! He's calling you to do good. But sometimes the good thing is the hard thing.

Try following Jesus' example. You might think that everything was easy for Him, but guess what? He felt the same tough feelings you feel! Loneliness? Yep. Fear? You bet. And He still chose to do good! He knew God's way is better than any other way. And if Jesus did it, He can help you do it too.

THOUGHT OF THE DAY

You can trust Jesus, because He knows how you feel.

PRAY TODAY

Dear Jesus, do You remember how hard it can be to make the right choice? Help me when I think I can't do it. Amen.

BUILD A HAPPY HOME

"If a house is divided against itself, that house cannot stand."

MARK 3:25 NIV

Everyone's home looks a little different. Do you have friends who have lots of brothers and sisters? Or none at all? Kids might live with their moms, dads, grandparents, uncles and aunts, foster parents, step-siblings, helpers, or some combination of those things. But God tells us that every home should have one thing in common: love. Love is like strong metal and sturdy bricks, building a home that can stand up to anything. Disagreements can't break it apart! Arguments can't knock it down. So pour love into your family every day. You're helping to build a home that will last!

THOUGHT OF THE DAY

Show love where you live.

PRAY TODAY

Dear God, help me to show love to each person in my family. I want our home to be strong and happy! Amen.

WELCOME TO GOD'S FAMILY!

Yes, it is through Christ we all have the right to come to the Father in one Spirit.

EPHESIANS 2:18 NCV

Have you ever made a secret club that only you and a few friends could belong to? Maybe it was just for girls. The people who could belong felt special, but others felt left out.

The Bible says Jesus gives everyone the right to come to God. We are all welcome to belong to God's family. Jesus doesn't leave anyone out. If you want to be with God, you can! That is because God loves each and every person. Each girl and boy is special to Him. Anyone who wants to join God's family is welcome!

THOUGHT OF THE DAY

You can be sure, so have no doubt, that Jesus never leaves anyone out!

PRAY TODAY

Dear God, I'm so glad that You welcome everyone into Your family. Thank You for loving me so much! Amen.

OBEY EACH DAY

But Jesus said, "Those who hear the teaching of God and obey it—they are the ones who are truly blessed."

LUKE 11:28 ICB

Moses was a great leader. But he wasn't always that way. One day, while Moses was tending sheep, God told him to go and challenge a powerful king. Moses was surprised and scared! He didn't like to talk in front of people, and he knew the king was dangerous. But God promised He would help Moses, so Moses obeyed. And because of that, Moses did great things!

God has a plan for your life too! When you pray, ask God to show you what to do each day. When you obey God like Moses did, you can do great things!

THOUGHT OF THE DAY

Sometimes God's ideas are surprising, like loving your enemies! Can you do that?

PRAY TODAY

Dear God, please help me obey You, even when You tell me to do something scary or surprising! Amen.

ROYAL KINDNESS

If you really keep the royal law found in Scripture, "Love your neighbor as yourself," you are doing right.

JAMES 2:8 NIV

Have you ever wanted to be a queen? When you follow God's Word, you can! The Bible tells us that when you treat others the way you'd like to be treated, you are following a "royal law." When you listen well and help friends solve problems, you're like King Solomon, who was full of wisdom. When you stand up for others who are in trouble, you're like Queen Esther, who spoke up and saved her people from an evil plot. Each day, find ways to put others first. You will be royally blessed!

THOUGHT OF THE DAY

What's something kind you'd like to hear from a friend? Say that to someone today!

PRAY TODAY

Dear God, help me remember to treat everyone with kindness and respect. I know we are all precious to You! Amen.

ALWAYS TOGETHER

"I assure you: Anyone who believes has eternal life."

JOHN 6:47 HCSB

God loves you so much. He never wants to be apart from you. And that's why He sent Jesus! Because of Jesus, everyone who wants to can be with God forever. What wonderful news!

When you invite Jesus to live in your heart, He stays there forever. You can never make a mistake bad enough to make Him leave. Nothing you say or do—and nothing you've said or done before—can keep you from God, and no one can take Him away from you. You will always be part of God's family. That's a promise you can count on!

THOUGHT OF THE DAY

God loves you—yesterday, today, and always!

PRAY TODAY

Dear God, I am so glad Your love is forever! Amen.

FILLED WITH GRACE

For by grace you have been saved through faith. And this is not your own doing; it is the gift of God.

EPHESIANS 2:8 ESV

Sometimes you get a reward for doing something well—like a trophy for winning a race. But you can have God's grace without doing anything at all! It's free, and it's the best gift ever.

Grace means that God cares for us, no matter what we do. And He loves us so much, He sent Jesus to save us. God's grace is for anyone who wants it! You don't have to wonder if you're "good enough." You don't have to work extra hard and hope that He chooses you. All you have to do is accept—and enjoy!—His wonderful gift.

THOUGHT OF THE DAY

You are enough for God, just because you're YOU.

PRAY TODAY

Dear God, thank You so much for Your grace. I love knowing I'm Your child forever. Amen.

YOU CAN DO ANYTHING

Then Jesus said to him . . . "Everything is possible to the one who believes."

MARK 9:23 HCSB

God promises to help you do great things when you trust Him. You don't have to be afraid to try something new—with God's help, you can do anything!

That doesn't mean everything will be easy. You may have to work hard to learn new things. It'll take courage to make new friends. You'll have to practice before you can play your instrument well or kick that winning soccer goal or draw a perfect spaceship. But God gives you strength, perseverance, and joy along the way! So don't give up. After all, God will never give up on you.

THOUGHT OF THE DAY

Believe in God, and He'll help you believe in yourself!

PRAY TODAY

Dear God, sometimes I get discouraged. Please help me remember that with You, I can do anything! Amen.

PUT OUT THE FIRE

Without wood, a fire will go out, and without gossip, quarreling will stop.

PROVERBS 26:20 NCV

Do you know what keeps a fire burning? Wood! If there is no more wood, a fire will go out. Today's Bible verse says that quarreling—or arguing—is like a burning fire. When we gossip or talk about others in unkind ways, it is like tossing more and more wood on a fire. It makes an argument get bigger and bigger. But if someone stops saying unkind or mean things, then the arguing stops. You can be a good friend and help put out "fiery" quarrels by using kind words instead of gossip.

THOUGHT OF THE DAY

Kind words cool off hot tempers!

PRAY TODAY

Dear God, please help me to use my words carefully. Help me say kind things instead of gossip. Amen.

WHOSE CHILD ARE YOU?

Dear friends, let us practice loving each other, for love comes from God and those who are loving and kind show that they are the children of God, and that they are getting to know him better.

1 JOHN 4:7 TLB

How do you show that you belong to your family? Do you look like your parents or your brothers or sisters? Do you all have the same last name? Do you all live in the same place?

We are all part of God's family. And the Bible tells us that there's a special way we can show it: be kind and loving! Look for ways to help others, share with them, listen to them, and be a good friend. When you do this, you're showing the world who your heavenly Father is!

THOUGHT OF THE DAY

How will you show someone you are in God's family today?

PRAY TODAY

Dear God, thank You for making me part of Your family. Please help me to practice loving others so they know I love You! Amen.

DO IT FOR JESUS!

". . . I tell you the truth, anything you did for even the least of my people here, you also did for me."

MATTHEW 25:40 NCV

Sometimes it's hard to put others first. But what if you imagine that you're actually serving Jesus? The Bible tells us that when we do something kind for someone else, it's as if we're doing it for Jesus! So when your sister begs you to share your toys, imagine it's Jesus sitting there. Try to see Him in everyone you meet—the new kid at school who looks lonely at recess, the older folks at church you could hold the door open for, or the homeless person who might need food. Showing kindness to other people is a great way to love Jesus.

THOUGHT OF THE DAY

How can you show kindness to someone new today?

PRAY TODAY

Dear Jesus, please help me remember that loving You means loving others too. Amen.

GOD'S GOOD GIFTS

Every good gift and every perfect gift is from above, and comes down from the Father of lights.

JAMES 1:17A NKJV

Don't you love receiving gifts? Maybe you also love giving gifts to those you love. Do you know that God loves to give His children good and perfect gifts? God's perfect gifts aren't just for birthdays or Christmas, and they never wear out or break. They are wonderful things like the love of your family and friends, the majesty of a golden sunset, the beauty of a starry sky, the amazing way you grow and learn new things. Look around and remember to thank God for all the good and perfect gifts He gives you each day!

THOUGHT OF THE DAY

Name some of the good gifts God has given you!

PRAY TODAY

Dear God, thank You for loving me so much and for giving me good and perfect gifts every day. Amen.

SHOW AND TELL

Little children, let us stop just saying we love people; let us really love them, and show it by our actions.

1 JOHN 3:18 TLB

Have you heard of show-and-tell? It's when you bring something—maybe a favorite toy—to your class and talk about it. If you just told your class about your special toy, but you didn't show it, they wouldn't see it. But if you just showed it to them, and didn't say anything about it, they wouldn't know much about it. Love is like that. We need to both show and tell people that we love them. Words are important, but showing our love by helping, sharing, being kind, and forgiving helps people know how much we love them.

THOUGHT OF THE DAY

To love others well, show and tell!

PRAY TODAY

Dear God, please help me to use both my words and my actions to let others know I love them. Amen.

DAY 156

A NEW YOU

Put on the new self, created to be like God in true righteousness and holiness.

EPHESIANS 4:24 NIV

Do you ever say, "That's just the way I am! I can't change." It is easy to keep doing things the same old way. But did you know that the Bible says you can "put on the new self"? You don't have to always lose your temper. You don't have to always have your own way. If you want to, you can choose to be different. With God's help, you can "put on the new self." Each morning, ask God to help you put on kindness, patience, and understanding. Then look for opportunities to practice being the new you!

THOUGHT OF THE DAY

What is one way you'd like to change and grow today?

PRAY TODAY

Dear God, sometimes I do or say things that aren't kind. Please help me to choose a different way. Amen.

DREAM BIG, TRUST GOD

Now glory be to God, who by his mighty power at work within us is able to do far more than we would ever dare to ask or even dream of—infinitely beyond our highest prayers, desires, thoughts, or hopes.

EPHESIANS 3:20 TLB

Larry likes pretending to be Larryboy—the most super of superheroes! And you probably like to pretend to do exciting things too! But guess what? You can do more than pretend. You can ask God to do mighty things through you. And He will!

He won't make you fly or turn invisible. But God can use you to change the world! Maybe He'll give you super courage to protect a sibling who is getting teased—or big ideas to help a cause you care about. He'll give you strength to work hard so you can accomplish your biggest dreams. Nothing is too amazing for God!

THOUGHT OF THE DAY

With God, you don't have to pretend. You just have to trust.

PRAY TODAY

Dear God, help me trust You so we can do big things together! Amen.

WORKING TOGETHER

Two people are better than one, because they get more done by working together.

ECCLESIASTES 4:9 NCV

What do you wish for when you have a big chore to do? A friend to help you out! What does your friend wish for when they have a problem to solve? You! When two buddies work together, they can get the job done in half the time. The work is easier, and then you both have more time to play! Look around. Is there someone who needs help? Lend them a hand. And when you have a job that seems tough to do, don't be afraid to ask for a little help. Working together is much better (and way more fun!) than working alone.

THOUGHT OF THE DAY

Who can you help today?

PRAY TODAY

Dear God, thank You for always helping me. Please remind me to work together with others! Amen.

PAST, PRESENT, AND FUTURE

But for those who honor the LORD, his love lasts forever, and his goodness endures for all generations.

PSALM 103:17 GNT

Have you ever looked at old family photos? Lots of things are different now! Clothes that your grandparents wore as children might look strange to you. Cars used to have more fancy details. Even hairstyles have changed—check out some pictures from the 1970s and '80s! People grow older, invent new things, and think new thoughts. But do you know what has always been the same, and will never, ever change? God's love. You've had it your whole life and you will never lose it. And there is enough for everyone—past, present, and future!

THOUGHT OF THE DAY

Today, tomorrow, yesterday, God's great love is here to stay.

PRAY TODAY

Dear God, I am so glad I will never lose Your love. Thank You for loving us all, every day, no matter what. Amen.

DAY 160

DOING IS IMPORTANT

But be doers of the word and not hearers only.

JAMES 1:22A HCSB

What if you read the words in a cookbook, but you never cooked anything? What if you got a toy for your birthday, but you just looked at the directions and never put it together? It's important to do what the words say!

In the same way, we should do something about what the Bible says. When Jesus says to "love your neighbor," we need to find ways to show love. When we hear a story that reminds us to forgive, we should learn to forgive others. Hearing is just one part of God's plan. Doing is important too!

THOUGHT OF THE DAY

What is one way you will do what the Bible says today?

PRAY TODAY

Dear God, thank You for the Bible. Please help me to not just listen to the words in it, but to do what it says. Amen.

YOU CAN BE ROYALTY

And if children, then heirs—heirs of God and fellow heirs with Christ.

ROMANS 8:17A ESV

Do you know that you can be part of a royal family? The Bible tells us that God is the King of the universe. And God says that if you love and trust Jesus, then you are also God's daughter! You are an heir of God, and you can have all of the wonderful gifts that God gives each of His children. You can have peace, joy, love, faith, answers to your prayers, and power to be strong when you feel weak. When you become part of God's family, God makes you His royal child!

THOUGHT OF THE DAY

What do you love about being in God's royal family?

PRAY TODAY

Dear God, thank You for welcoming me into Your royal family. Help me to live like a child of the King. Amen.

ALWAYS GIVE THANKS

Rejoice always! Pray constantly. Give thanks in everything, for this is God's will for you in Christ Jesus.

1 THESSALONIANS 5:16–18 HCSB

You know to say "thank you" when someone does something nice for you. But do you know that the Bible says we should give thanks all the time?

Sometimes giving thanks can be hard. What if it rains when you want to play outside? Or you get sick and can't be with friends? What if your best friend moves away? At those times, you can give thanks that God is always with you. You can also give thanks that God promises to love and help you no matter what happens. Why not thank Him for that today?

THOUGHT OF THE DAY

What are three things you can thank God for today?

PRAY TODAY

Dear God, I'm so glad You've promised to always be with me. Please help me remember to give You thanks every day. Amen.

CLEAN AGAIN

If we tell Him our sins, He is faithful and we can depend on Him to forgive us of our sins. He will make our lives clean from all sin.

1 JOHN 1:9 NLV

When you make a mistake drawing or writing with a pencil, you can use an eraser to erase the mistake and start over. When you get dirt on your clothes, you can wash them and make them clean again. But what happens if you do something wrong or hurt someone with your words or actions? God says that if we tell Him about the wrong things we do and ask Him to forgive us, He will! He promises to make our lives clean again, so we can start over and do better the next time.

THOUGHT OF THE DAY

Soap can clean your hands, but only God can clean your heart!

PRAY TODAY

Dear God, thank You for loving me so much. Please help me to always come to You for forgiveness. Amen.

BE GOD'S HANDS

Never walk away from someone who deserves help; your hand is God's hand for that person.

PROVERBS 3:27 MSG

Have you ever thought about how very special your hands are? You can draw with them, build with them, even use sign language to "talk" with them. But there is something even more special you can do with your hands—the Bible says you can be God's hands. How? When you help someone, when you comfort someone, when you pat someone on the back to encourage them, when you make a gift to let someone know you love them, you are showing them that God loves them too—you are being God's hands!

THOUGHT OF THE DAY

How can you be God's hands today?

PRAY TODAY

Dear God, please help me use my hands to show others that You love them. Amen.

HAVE A PARTY HEART!

A cheerful heart has a continual feast.

PROVERBS 15:15B HCSB

Who doesn't love a party? It feels great to celebrate! And God says you can feel that way every day. Just develop a Party Heart!

A Party Heart is a heart that chooses cheerfulness. You can turn your heart into a Party Heart by always looking for reasons to be happy. They can be big, like winning a prize, or small, like finding a ladybug. When your heart is busy finding happy things, you won't have time to dwell on things that don't go your way. Your cheerful heart will just go right on partying!

THOUGHT OF THE DAY

Who has time for gloom and doom when your heart's a party room?

PRAY TODAY

Dear God, You're invited to the party in my heart—let's celebrate! Amen.

THE BEST WAY TO BE

"Treat others just as you want to be treated."

LUKE 6:31 CEV

How do you treat others? If someone is unkind to you, are you unkind to them? If someone won't share, are you selfish too? If someone pushes you, do you push them back?

Sometimes, we treat others the way they treat us—if they are mean, so are we. But Jesus teaches us something different. He says we should treat others the way we want to be treated. No matter what they do! So if you want others to be kind and share with you, you should be kind and share with them. It's the very best way to be!

THOUGHT OF THE DAY

If you want others to be kind to you, learn to treat them with kindness too!

PRAY TODAY

Dear God, help me to follow Your teaching and to treat others the way I want to be treated. Amen.

WHAT DO YOU DO?

God has given each of you a gift from his great variety of spiritual gifts. Use them well to serve one another.

1 PETER 4:10 NLT

The Bible says God gives each person "spiritual gifts." That means things they are especially good at, which can be used to serve God and help people. So how do you find yours? Look for things that come easily to you, or ways of helping that you really enjoy. Do you love to sing in front of people? Do you jump in when work needs to get done, or do you always have a joke to share with a sad friend? Is it easy to encourage others? Ask God to reveal your special gifts. Then use them to share His love!

THOUGHT OF THE DAY

Ask a grown-up what they think you're good at—it could be a clue to discovering your spiritual gifts!

PRAY TODAY

Dear God, what have You created me to do for You? Help me find the gifts You've given me! Amen.

PRAISING GOD

I will bless the LORD at all times; His praise shall continually be in my mouth.

PSALM 34:1 AMP

When we praise God, we remember how great He is. God created the universe and every living thing. He is wiser and more powerful than anyone. God never makes mistakes, and He always loves us. That is still true when things get hard.

When you are afraid or lonely, sick or sad, it is good to remember that God is always with you. He will never leave you, and He always wants to help you. When we praise God, we remember that nothing is too hard for Him. Praise helps us love and trust God more, no matter what happens.

THOUGHT OF THE DAY

What are some things you can praise God for today?

PRAY TODAY

Dear God, I'm so glad You are so powerful. You are greater than anything, and Your love lasts forever. Amen.

ENCOURAGE EACH OTHER

You must encourage one another each day.

HEBREWS 3:13A CEV

Sometimes we need a friend to help us out or lift our spirits. Maybe you are having a hard time learning something new. Or you are feeling sad because someone hurt your feelings. Maybe you made a big mistake or did something you weren't supposed to do. Those are times when you need to be encouraged. You need to hear someone say, "It will be OK." "I understand." "Let me help you." And there are times when you need to encourage someone else too. God tells us to encourage each other. Why not try to be an encourager today?

THOUGHT OF THE DAY

What are some ways you can be an encourager today?

PRAY TODAY

Dear God, I'm so glad You love and encourage me. Please help me to find ways to encourage others today. Amen.

GOD WILL BE WITH YOU

"Be strong! Be courageous! Do not be afraid of them! For the Lord your God will be with you. He will neither fail you nor forsake you."

DEUTERONOMY 31:6 TLB

When Joshua became the new leader of the Israelites, he faced many enemies. God did not make the enemies go away, but He gave Joshua a wonderful promise. He promised to always be with and help Joshua. Sometimes you will face scary things too. Maybe you will have to speak up when you feel shy. You might have to admit that you did something wrong. You may have to move or make new friends. God promises to be with you too! When you feel afraid, God will always be with you. You can count on Him!

THOUGHT OF THE DAY

What are some things that make you feel afraid?

PRAY TODAY

Dear God, thank You for promising to always be with me. When I feel afraid, help me to remember that You are with me. Amen.

ALWAYS THERE

"Do not be afraid or discouraged. For the Lord your God is with you wherever you go."

JOSHUA 1:9B NLT

Have you ever felt like you were all alone? Maybe you weren't sure what to do and felt scared, or you were discouraged because you made a mistake. God understands. He knows how you feel whether you are happy or sad, excited or worried, feeling brave or feeling afraid. And God is always right where you are, no matter where you go. You never have to feel embarrassed to share how you feel or ask Him for help. He cares for you, and He wants you to know that He will never leave you.

THOUGHT OF THE DAY

God is always there, and He will always care.

PRAY TODAY

Thank You, God, for understanding how I feel. I'm so glad You are always with me. Amen.

A SAFE PLACE

You are my hiding place and my shield; I hope in your word.

PSALM 119:114 NCV

What makes you feel safe? A hug from someone you love? Holding a favorite toy? How about saying a prayer?

Today's verse tells us that God is a protector. Sometimes people go through hard times and the world feels scary. Thinking about God's good promises can help you feel safe. His love never goes away, no matter what's happening around us or what mistakes we make. So when you feel nervous or lonely or angry or sad, remember that you are wrapped in God's love. He is a safe place that goes wherever you go.

THOUGHT OF THE DAY

God is always with you—you can't accidentally leave Him at home!

PRAY TODAY

Dear God, I am glad You're with me all the time. Please hold me close when I feel scared. Amen.

GOOD IN, GOOD OUT

"A good man brings good things out of the good stored up in him."

MATTHEW 12:35A NIV

Grown-ups like to tell kids to be nice to each other. It's pretty important! But did you know that showing yourself kindness is just as important as being kind to others? You are a precious child of God! When you do something well, celebrate! When you mess up, forgive yourself. When you feel overwhelmed, ask for help. Then as you store up all that kindness inside you, something cool will happen: It'll start to overflow! When you've filled yourself with good things, you can't help but share them with everyone around you.

THOUGHT OF THE DAY

What's a kind thing you can do for yourself today?

PRAY TODAY

Dear God, help me remember to be kind to myself and those around me. We are all so important to You! Amen.

GOD'S GOT A PLAN

"Who knows? Maybe you were made queen for just such a time as this."

ESTHER 4:14 MSG

Sometimes it seems like God makes no sense. The people in the Bible probably thought that sometimes! After all, Jesus borrowed a kid's lunch to feed five thousand people, Daniel got thrown in a den of lions, and Esther, a poor peasant girl, became queen of Persia! But there's one thing all those wild stories have in common: God had a good plan for each person. And God has a good plan for you too! Whatever is going on in your life, God is right there with you. And He's got great things in store for you.

THOUGHT OF THE DAY

When you don't know what to do, trust in God's good plan for you.

PRAY TODAY

Dear God, thank You for loving me. Help me remember that Your plans are good, even if my days feel hard. Amen.

GET CURIOUS

Don't let your spirit rush to be angry, for anger abides in the heart of fools.

ECCLESIASTES 7:9 HCSB

Everyone gets mad sometimes. But when we get too mad too fast, that's a problem. It can make us do or say hurtful things. So instead of rushing into anger, see if you can take your feelings in a different direction: curiosity.

First, take a big breath in and out. Then ask yourself some questions. Why did that person say that? Why didn't I get what I wanted? What does my body feel like? How might the other person feel? How can God help me? Asking questions is a good way to slow down and find a solution that can help, not hurt!

THOUGHT OF THE DAY

When anger makes you want to cry, take a breath and then ask "why?"

PRAY TODAY

Dear God, I don't like getting so mad. Help me slow down next time and figure out how to feel better. Amen.

THANK YOU!

Give thanks to the LORD, for he is good! His faithful love endures forever.

PSALM 136:1 NLT

People love to receive thank-you notes when they send a gift. A thoughtful note lets them know you enjoy their gift! God likes to know you enjoy His good gifts too. So why not send Him a note?

Draw a picture of something that makes you happy and thank God while you're coloring it. Do you have a funny pet? Did you get to play in the sunshine today or splash in big rain puddles? God loves to fill your days with good things. Thank Him for a few of them today!

THOUGHT OF THE DAY

Thanking God each day makes you feel good too!

PRAY TODAY

Dear God, what a beautiful world You've made! Thank You for today! Amen.

WISE WORDS

When you're kind to others, you help yourself; when you're cruel to others, you hurt yourself.

PROVERBS 11:17 MSG

Almost three thousand years ago, a wise king named Solomon collected true sayings and wrote them down. The book of Proverbs contains many of these words of wisdom. In fact, today's Bible verse is one of Solomon's sayings!

You might think that being kind only helps the person you are kind to. But a wise person knows that others often treat you the way you treat them. If you want others to be kind to you, be kind to them! It was true three thousand years ago and it's still true today!

THOUGHT OF THE DAY

Be a friend to have a friend!

PRAY TODAY

Dear God, thank You for the wisdom You show me in the Bible. Please help me to follow wise words. Amen.

HANGING OUT WITH GOD

Let all that I am wait quietly before God, for my hope is in him.

PSALM 62:5 NLT

Even though God is always around, it can be hard to feel like you're "hanging out" together. There are so many other things to pay attention to!

That's why so many people in the Bible—and today—set aside time to be alone with God. Moses even went to the top of a mountain! But you don't have to break out your climbing shoes. Can you take a few minutes right after you wake up, or before you go to bed? Spending time alone with God each day will help you remember that He's your very best friend.

THOUGHT OF THE DAY

If just praying seems too hard, have a Bible story in mind to talk about!

PRAY TODAY

Dear God, please help me find time to spend with You. I want our friendship to be really strong! Amen.

A LOVE THAT'S FOREVER

Give thanks to the Lord, for he is good; his love endures forever.

PSALM 118:29 NIV

Sometimes we make bad choices and feel embarrassed. Or we feel disappointed about something that happened, and we might even get mad at God. But guess what? None of that can change God's love. His love is stronger than our anger. It's big enough to hold our joy, our sadness, our confusion, and everything in between. You can come to God with any feelings or questions, because He loves to help you. Don't worry about losing God's love. It has always been there for you, and it's never going away.

THOUGHT OF THE DAY

God loves to love you. He won't ever stop!

PRAY TODAY

Dear God, thank You for loving me forever, no matter what happens. That makes me so glad! Amen.

JUST BE YOU!

And a voice from heaven said, "You are my dearly loved Son, and you bring me great joy."

MARK 1:11 NLT

Jesus brought joy to God just by being who He was. That's how you bring joy to God too! He created you with your special mix of gifts, needs, interests, and personality. He doesn't want you to try to be anyone else. Instead, be true to yourself!

What does that mean? Be proud of the things you enjoy and ask for help when you need it. Do you like to paint? Paint beautiful pictures! Is reading hard for you? Ask an older friend or sibling for help. It brings God joy when you express who you are!

THOUGHT OF THE DAY

Be who God made you to be!

PRAY TODAY

Dear God, please help me be proud of how You made me. I want to bring You joy! Amen.

DOING WHAT GOD WANTS

"Seek first God's kingdom and what God wants. Then all your other needs will be met as well."

MATTHEW 6:33 NCV

One day Jesus listened to some people who were worried. "What about us?" they asked. "How will we get what we need?" Jesus told them that if they did what God wanted first, they could stop worrying because God would take care of them. That's good advice for us too. The Bible teaches us what God wants us to do: be kind, share what you have, make everyone feel welcomed, help people who are hurting or sad, pray for others. Doing what God wants first takes care of everyone's needs—including yours!

THOUGHT OF THE DAY

What is something God wants you to do today?

PRAY TODAY

Dear God, please help me to do what You want and to trust You for all I need. Amen.

SAY IT WITH A SMILE

Happiness makes a person smile, but sadness can break a person's spirit.

PROVERBS 15:13 NCV

When you smile at someone, it makes them want to smile back at you! And it is hard to stay mad or sad when you are smiling. Smiling is a good way to help someone else feel better too. A smile says, "I like you." Or it can say, "I want to be your friend." It can even say, "I'm sorry. Let's try again." If you want to feel better and help others feel better too, put a smile on your face. It is a great way to share a little happiness.

THOUGHT OF THE DAY

Try putting a smile on your face today. It can help you show what you want to say!

PRAY TODAY

Dear God, please help me to share kindness and joy today by wearing a smile. Amen.

HAPPINESS FROM THE INSIDE

I'm happy from the inside out, and from the outside in, I'm firmly formed.

PSALM 16:9A MSG

A smile often means a happy heart! But sometimes people put on a smile when they feel angry inside. Or they act happy when they are really sad. Or they hide their scared feelings by acting extra loud and silly. They think they need to pretend so others will like them.

When it's hard for you to feel happy all the way through, ask God to help you understand why. Find a grown-up who will listen to your feelings, and help you find good solutions. You are precious to God. He wants your outside happiness to come from inside joy!

THOUGHT OF THE DAY

How does your inside feel?

PRAY TODAY

Dear God, please help me pay attention to my inside feelings, and please give me Your joy! Amen.

LEAD WITH YOUR ACTIONS

In every way be an example of doing good deeds. When you teach, do it with honesty and seriousness.

TITUS 2:7 NCV

The best leaders don't just tell others what to do—they lead with their actions! And God wants you to lead people to Him. So be sure to choose good, kind actions that show people what God's love looks like! Treat people with respect, and they'll understand how to treat others that way too. When you keep your promises, you show what it means to be trustworthy, even when it's hard. When you tell the truth, others can see what honesty looks like. How will you lead with your actions today?

THOUGHT OF THE DAY

You can be a leader by following God's ways!

PRAY TODAY

Dear God, help me choose good actions so I can be a good leader who points people to You! Amen.

GOD'S GREAT LOVE

This is what real love is: It is not our love for God; it is God's love for us. He sent his Son to die in our place to take away our sins.

1 JOHN 4:10 NCV

Have you ever heard the word *sin*? Sin means that we do what we want instead of what God wants. Every person sins, and our sin moves us away from God. But God loves us and wants us to be close to Him, so He made a wonderful plan. God sent Jesus! Jesus never sinned. He showed us how to follow God by loving others and trusting God's words. He even took the punishment for our sins! When we accept God's love for us in Jesus, God takes away our sins. Then we can live with Him forever. What amazing love!

THOUGHT OF THE DAY

God loves you more than you can ever imagine! Will you choose to love Him back?

PRAY TODAY

Dear God, thank You for loving me and for sending Your Son, Jesus, to take away my sin. Help me to learn to love You more every day. Amen.

HEAVEN IS AN AMAZING PLACE!

"No eye has seen, no ear has heard, and no mind has imagined what God has prepared for those who love him."

1 CORINTHIANS 2:9B NLT

Do you ever think about what heaven is like? The Bible gives us a few clues. We know that it is a place God has prepared for those who love Him. There is no sadness or suffering in heaven, and God is there. But the Bible also says we can't even imagine how wonderful heaven is. Will there be angels? Will the streets be made of gold and the gates of sparkling jewels? No one knows. We can only trust that it will be like nothing we've ever seen, and will be filled with God's wonderful, unending love.

THOUGHT OF THE DAY

Heaven is an amazing place. It is filled with God's love and grace!

PRAY TODAY

Dear God, thank You for loving me so much and for preparing heaven, an amazing place where I can live with You forever. Amen.

GOD WANTS TO HELP YOU

Jesus looked at them and said, "With man this is impossible, but with God all things are possible."

MATTHEW 19:26 NIV

Have you ever wanted to tell the truth, but you told a lie instead? Maybe you wanted to obey your parents, but then you didn't. Have you ever had a habit you wanted to stop, but you just couldn't keep from doing it? Sometimes wanting to do the right thing isn't enough. You just can't do it by yourself! Fortunately, the Bible promises that when we can't do what we want, God is there to help us. When you aren't strong enough to do the right thing, ask God to help you. With God all things are possible!

THOUGHT OF THE DAY

What are some things you want God to help you with?

PRAY TODAY

Dear God, I can't always do the things I should. Please remind me to ask You when I need help. Amen.

FRIENDS STICK TOGETHER

But Ruth said, "Do not urge me to leave you or to return from following you. For where you go I will go, and where you lodge I will lodge. Your people shall be my people, and your God my God."

RUTH 1:16 ESV

In our Bible verse today, Naomi and Ruth have been through some hard times, and Naomi has decided to go back to her old home in Bethlehem. She urges Ruth to return to her own home in Moab. But Ruth loves Naomi, and she wants to stay with her. They are very good friends, and friends don't give up on each other when times get hard. They stick around! Friends encourage each other when they're sad or lonely. They listen, ask questions, and find ways to help. We all need good friends—in good times and bad!

THOUGHT OF THE DAY

Who is a good friend to you? What are some ways you can be a good friend?

PRAY TODAY

Dear God, thank You for my good friends. Please help me to be a good friend who listens and cares. Amen.

GOD MADE YOU

For you created my inmost being; you knit me together in my mother's womb.

PSALM 139:13 NIV

Do you know that you are a work of art? The Bible says that God created you carefully and with love. He made you to be just who you are. He gave you talents and abilities. He thought about what kind of hair and eyes you have, how tall you are, the color of your skin, and the way your mind works. Think about all the amazing things you can do! Realize that you are the only person who is just like you. Then take time each day to thank God for how wonderfully He has made you!

THOUGHT OF THE DAY

What do you like about how God made you?

PRAY TODAY

Dear God, thank You for making me just the way I am and for loving me so much. Amen.

GOD WILL FORGIVE

"I will forgive their wrongdoing, and I will never again remember their sins."

HEBREWS 8:12 CSB

When you say mean words, treat someone unkindly, or ruin something that belongs to them, it can make you feel unhappy. That unhappy feeling is because you know you have done something wrong. The Bible calls this "wrongdoing" or "sin." God understands and He will help you to do better. That's why He wants you to ask Him for forgiveness. When you tell God what you have done wrong, and ask him to forgive you and help you make things right, He promises He will! God loves you and wants to help you learn and grow.

THOUGHT OF THE DAY

When you do something wrong, remember God is there to forgive and help you!

PRAY TODAY

Dear God, I'm sorry that I don't always do what's right. Please help me to ask You to forgive me and help me do better. Amen.

BEAUTIFUL FRIENDS

You made man a little lower than the angels. And you crowned him with glory and honor.

PSALM 8:5 ICB

No two people are exactly alike. Look around! God filled His world with people of different sizes, colors, interests, and abilities.

You might know someone who needs a little extra help. People who need help learning often have a special helper. People who need help getting around might have a wheelchair or crutches. People who need help seeing can wear glasses or use a special cane. Someone who looks, sounds, or acts differently from you can be just as good a friend as anyone else! So be sure to include all kinds of people when you're making friends. It'll make your world even more beautiful!

THOUGHT OF THE DAY

Sometimes people feel sensitive about differences. Be sure to ask questions with kindness!

PRAY TODAY

Dear God, thank You for making all sorts of amazing people! Amen.

COUNT ON GOD

Only God gives inward peace, and I depend on him.

PSALM 62:5 CEV

Sometimes you wake up, and the sun is shining. Then later at the park, rain pours down and you wish you'd brought an umbrella! Or you go to bed under a clear starry sky, but wake up to your yard hiding under a blanket of snow. We can't always know what we'll see outside our window. But one thing we can always count on is God's love. He will never leave you. He loves to hear your prayers. He is patient, gentle, and kind, and nothing is too hard for Him. God is the same in sunshine, rain, or snow!

THOUGHT OF THE DAY

Count on God and never fear because His love is always near!

PRAY TODAY

Dear God, thank You for never changing. I'm so glad I can count on You. Amen.

TELLING THE TRUTH

You want me to be completely truthful, so teach me wisdom.

PSALM 51:6 NCV

When you do something wrong, make a mistake, or break a rule, you might feel scared. You worry about getting into trouble or having someone upset with you. Then you have to make a choice: to tell the truth or a lie. God wants us to tell the truth even when it's hard to do. When you tell the truth, people learn they can trust you and believe what you say. And telling the truth has another benefit—you feel better about yourself. You know you've been brave enough to do the right thing!

THOUGHT OF THE DAY

When you learn to say what's true, others learn they can count on you!

PRAY TODAY

Dear God, please help me to be wise and choose to tell the truth, even when it is hard to do. Amen.

POWER TO SHARE

Do not withhold good from those who deserve it when it's in your power to help them.

PROVERBS 3:27 NLT

If you have a cookie and your friend has none, you could break your cookie in half and share it. If you have two toys and your buddy doesn't have one, you could share and play together. The Bible says that it's always good to give and share when we have something that others need. Sharing might feel hard to do, but it's actually a special power. It makes friendships stronger and helps others! You can use this special power any time you want—just look around and see if there's someone you can help. Then go save the day!

THOUGHT OF THE DAY

The power to share will show that you care.

PRAY TODAY

Dear God, I am so thankful for all You have given me. Please help me use my power to share with others. Amen.

GOD IS THERE TO HELP

Depend on the Lord and his strength. Always go to him for help.

1 CHRONICLES 16:11 ICB

Isn't it great when a friend helps you solve a problem or learn something new? Doesn't it feel good to know that your parents are there to help you when you don't know what to do? God is a good Friend and Father, and He wants to help you too. God has more wisdom and strength than any person in the world, and He is always there, even when you feel alone. The Bible tells us that when we take our problems to God, He is happy to help us.

THOUGHT OF THE DAY

What is something you will ask God to help you with today?

PRAY TODAY

Dear God, I'm so glad You are always there to help me. Thank You for loving me so much. Amen.

YOU CAN BE BRAVE

"Be strong! Be courageous! Do not be afraid of them! For the Lord your God will be with you. He will neither fail you nor forsake you."

DEUTERONOMY 31:6 TLB

God led His people to a wonderful new land, but they were afraid to go in. Have you ever felt afraid to go somewhere new? Maybe you went to school, and it was hard to say goodbye to your grown-up. Maybe you had to sleep in a strange room on a family trip. Or maybe you've moved to a new home, and nothing feels like it used to. Different places can make you feel different feelings. But God promises that no matter where you are, He is always with you. He can give you courage, calmness, and joy wherever you go.

THOUGHT OF THE DAY

In every place, you'll find God's grace!

PRAY TODAY

Dear God, I am so glad You are always with me, and that You will help me to be brave. Amen.

CREATIVE WAITING

A wise person is patient.

PROVERBS 19:11A ICB

Waiting is not easy. Especially when you're waiting for something you really want! But the Bible tells us that wise people are patient—that means they have a good attitude while they wait. Try doing something fun to help. If you're counting the days until Christmas or a vacation, cross off days on a calendar or tear links off a paper chain. If you have a playdate later in the day, spend your time drawing a picture to give to your friend when you see them. Use your creative brain to fill the time when you're waiting. It may make patience a bit more fun!

THOUGHT OF THE DAY

What do you like to do? How can that help you next time you need to be patient?

PRAY TODAY

Dear God, please help me think of ways to make waiting a little easier, and fun too! Amen.

BE HONORABLE

Do things in such a way that everyone can see you are honorable.

ROMANS 12:17B NLT

Being honorable means choosing to do the right thing, even when it is hard. If you break the rules or make a choice that isn't the best, it's tempting to hide, argue, or even lie about it. But God can help you be honorable instead. Pray for courage—it takes bravery to admit when you made a mistake! Then pray for patience—it might take some time to make things right. You may need to pick up your toys like you promised or fix something that broke. Finally, thank God for His loving help. When you're honorable, friends and family can believe what you say. And that makes everyone happier!

THOUGHT OF THE DAY

Who in your life do you think is honorable? Why?

PRAY TODAY

Dear God, please give me the courage to be honorable each day. Amen.

WHAT ARE YOU LOOKING FOR?

The one who searches for what is good finds favor, but if someone looks for trouble, it will come to him.

PROVERBS 11:27 HCSB

Do you know that people usually find what they're looking for? Not always with lost toys, but with goodness. If you look for things to be mad about, you can find them. If you look for reasons to be sad, you can probably find them too. But the opposite is also true. If you look for reasons to be happy, you can find them as well. Looking for what is good brings joy because you see how much there is to be thankful for! If you're feeling down, try searching for good things, like things you love about your life. Before you know it, you will be feeling better!

THOUGHT OF THE DAY

Name five things that you are thankful for today.

PRAY TODAY

Dear God, You have blessed me in so many ways. Please help me to always be thankful. Amen.

PEACEFUL FRIENDSHIPS

It is good and pleasant when God's people live together in peace!

PSALM 133:1 NCV

What kinds of people do you like to be around? Loud and exciting? Quiet and thoughtful? A bit of both? All friendships are different, but the best friendships are peaceful ones.

Peace means no matter what you do, you find ways to be kind to one another. If you get upset with a friend, you don't yell or fight—you talk about it. Nobody tells lies or says mean things. Instead, you only say good things to AND about each other! God says that when you fill your friendships with peace, you'll have so much more fun!

THOUGHT OF THE DAY

The key to good friendships is not hard to find. It's the peace that you feel when you choose to be kind!

PRAY TODAY

Dear God, if my friends and I disagree, help me to always make the choice that will lead to peace. Amen.

BUILD ENDURANCE

Let us run with endurance the race that is set before us.

HEBREWS 12:1B ESV

Endurance" is a big word that means not giving up. That's not so easy when you're tired, frustrated, or bored. But when you keep going even when it's hard, you get stronger and more confident! When you practice an instrument, you get to play beautiful music. If you mess up a painting and try again, you get better at art. And when you keep working to make new friends, learn new things, and trust God, you grow in wonderful ways! When things get hard, ask God for extra strength. He'll help you endure, so you can enjoy the rewards!

THOUGHT OF THE DAY

God will never give up on you!

PRAY TODAY

Dear God, Sometimes I feel like giving up. Please give me strength and endurance instead! Amen.

WAIT AND TRUST

Wait for the LORD; be strong, and let your heart take courage; wait for the LORD!

PSALM 27:14 ESV

Joseph was put in jail for something he didn't do. But instead of getting angry at God, he patiently trusted God to help him. One day, Joseph helped two other prisoners understand their dreams. When the king heard about Joseph's special gift, he freed him! Then Joseph became a powerful leader too. Joseph waited for God's timing, and it was perfect. Waiting for God takes courage. It means you trust that God is in charge, and you look for chances to use your gifts. Then, when the time is right, you'll be ready for whatever God has planned!

THOUGHT OF THE DAY

What is something you want to do? How can you bravely wait for it?

PRAY TODAY

Dear God, waiting is hard. Please help me remember that trusting You is a brave choice! Amen.

FOLLOWING JESUS

"Follow Me," Jesus told them, "and I will make you fish for people!" Immediately they left their nets and followed Him.

MARK 1:17-18 HCSB

When Jesus asked the fishermen, Simon and Andrew, to follow Him, they decided to do it. They made up their minds to do what Jesus asked. Because of that, Jesus taught them how to live and helped them to follow God. Today, we can't see Jesus like Simon and Andrew did, but He still wants us to follow Him. You can follow Jesus by reading His words in the Bible and doing what He says. Just like Simon and Andrew, you can be one of Jesus' disciples. He loves you and wants you to follow Him!

THOUGHT OF THE DAY

Follow Jesus every day by learning what He has to say!

PRAY TODAY

Dear Jesus, thank You for Your words in the Bible. Please help me to follow You each day. Amen.

HOW WOULD YOU FEEL?

If you really keep the royal law found in Scripture, "Love your neighbor as yourself," you are doing right.

JAMES 2:8 NIV

Have you ever wondered if you're doing the right thing? The Bible gives us a special key we can use to always know. Ask yourself: How would I feel?

Nervous about talking to someone who's lonely at recess? Ask yourself how you'd feel if you were left out and someone invited you to play. Unsure about sharing your extra cookie? Think about how happy you are when a friend shares with you. When you can imagine yourself in someone else's situation, it's easier to know how God wants you to act!

THOUGHT OF THE DAY

God's way isn't a mystery: show love to the folks you see!

PRAY TODAY

Dear God, each day is a new chance to be kind. Help me to love others like I love myself. Amen.

WHERE IS GOD?

No one has ever seen God; if we love one another, God abides in us and his love is perfected in us.

1 JOHN 4:12 ESV

Do you ever wish you could see God the way you see friends and family? The Bible says that even though no one can see Him, He can shine through us when we love each other!

God's love is perfect. So when we try to love like Him—like letting others go first, encouraging our friends, helping without asking for anything in return, and comforting those who are sad—we show people what God looks like. So share some love today. And watch how your favorite people love you too. Can you see God?

THOUGHT OF THE DAY

The more we share God's love, the more we have to give! That's perfect love!

PRAY TODAY

Dear God, Help me share Your perfect love so others can see what You're like!

DO THE RIGHT THING

He grants a treasure of common sense to the honest. He is a shield to those who walk with integrity.

PROVERBS 2:7 NLT

Life is full of rules, isn't it? If someone sees you breaking a rule, you might get in trouble. But what if no one knows? What if you feel like breaking a rule, and you think no one will notice? Don't do it! God sees, and He wants you to make good choices.

When you do the right thing, even when no one notices, that's called integrity. Maybe you tell the truth even when lying is easier. You clean your mess because you promised to, even if no one is watching. When you live with integrity, you can be proud of yourself every day!

THOUGHT OF THE DAY

Integrity is a gift you give to yourself.

PRAY TODAY

Dear God, sometimes I get tired of following rules. Help me choose integrity even when I don't feel like it. Amen.

TALKING AND LISTENING

There is a time for everything. . . . a time to be silent and a time to speak.

ECCLESIASTES 3:1A, 7B NIV

Do you have a hard time waiting your turn to tell everyone your stories or ideas? Or maybe you have a hard time speaking up? Maybe you'd rather listen to a story than tell one. People feel differently about talking in front of others, but God tells us there are times when it's important to be quiet and times when it's important to talk. It is good to know the difference. When you're in school or at church and someone is teaching you, be sure you're a good listener. When you have something important to share, be sure to speak up!

THOUGHT OF THE DAY

What is easier for you—talking or listening?

PRAY TODAY

Thank You, God, for always listening to me. Help me to be a good listener too. Amen.

COMMON COURTESY

Remind them . . . to avoid quarreling, to be gentle, and to show perfect courtesy toward all people.

TITUS 3:1A, 2B ESV

The Bible tells us to show courtesy—or good manners—to all people. That's because each person is important to God. So remember to say thank you whenever someone helps you, whether it's your grandma, your best friend, or the server at a restaurant! Try holding the door open for the person behind you when you go into a store or your classroom. Be sure to knock before you go into your sibling's room—that shows them you respect their privacy! Good manners help you show God's love every day.

THOUGHT OF THE DAY

Don't make manners something rare. Common courtesy shows you care!

PRAY TODAY

Dear God, it's cool that I can show Your love just by being polite! Help me remember my good manners every day. Amen.

DAY 209

EXTRA PEACE

Now may the Lord of peace himself give you peace at all times in every way. The Lord be with you all.

2 THESSALONIANS 3:16 ESV

Peace is one of God's greatest gifts. It can help you feel calm, confident, and even hopeful when things don't go your way.

Sometimes it's hard to find peace. After all, it's normal to feel upset when you don't get what you want. So try asking God to give you an extra helping of peace at extra hard times. He never runs out, and He loves to give His children good things. And a peaceful heart is the very best thing!

THOUGHT OF THE DAY

A trusting heart is a peaceful heart.

PRAY TODAY

Dear God, thank You for the gift of peace, and thank You that I can always ask for more! Amen.

JESUS BRINGS JOY

How we laughed and sang for joy. And the other nations said, "What amazing things the Lord has done for them."

PSALM 126:2 TLB

What makes you happy? Is it getting something you want for your birthday? Or getting to go somewhere special? Happiness usually depends on what happens to us. But this verse talks about joy, and joy isn't quite the same as happiness. It's better! Joy is a gift from Jesus. When we understand that Jesus loves us all the time, we experience joy. When we believe that Jesus forgives us and takes care of us every day, that gives us joy. Joy helps you feel hopeful no matter what happens, because joy depends on Jesus—and Jesus never changes!

THOUGHT OF THE DAY

Can you name something Jesus has done that gives you joy?

PRAY TODAY

Dear Jesus, thank You for loving me and promising You'll always be with me. You fill my heart with joy! Amen.

CHOOSE FAITH

I have chosen the way of faithfulness; I set your rules before me.

PSALM 119:30 ESV

King David made a very good choice. He decided that he wanted to have faith in God and remember His rules. But King David wasn't perfect. Sometimes he was selfish and made up his own rules instead. Sometimes he ignored people who reminded him to follow God! But each time he made mistakes, he chose to return to God and ask forgiveness. Then he tried again. You can do that too! God doesn't expect you to get everything right. But when you ask forgiveness and keep trying, God will grow your faith. You can choose God over and over, just like King David!

THOUGHT OF THE DAY

The only way your faith will grow is by choosing God wherever you go.

PRAY TODAY

Dear God, please help me remember Your rules. Thank You that I can always come back to You if I make mistakes. Amen.

TRUST ONLY GOD

"But blessed are those who trust in the LORD and have made the LORD their hope and confidence."

JEREMIAH 17:7 NLT

Larryboy wears a fancy mask and a cape, but he knows those things are just part of a costume. He puts his trust in God instead. And that's good! A costume can rip or shrink in the dryer or even get lost! But God never changes.

If you are scared to talk in front of your class, God has courage to give you. If you're missing friends or family, He has love and comfort for you. If you worry about what will happen tomorrow, His peace can calm you. Put your trust in God and He will always help you.

THOUGHT OF THE DAY

Is there something you can trust God with today? Ask for His help!

PRAY TODAY

Dear God, please help me trust You with every problem. I want to feel confident in Your strength! Amen.

BRING OUT THE BEST

Look for the best in each other, and always do your best to bring it out.

1 THESSALONIANS 5:15 MSG

Don't you love it when someone sees the best in you? Maybe your mom says, "You're such a good helper!" Maybe a teacher says, "You took turns at recess—what a good friend!" Maybe a neighbor says, "You always make me smile!" Did you know that you can bring out the best in others too? Notice when someone does something kind and say something about it! When a friend makes a mistake, be quick to forgive. Say caring words to someone who's sad. Speak up for someone who feels left out. Use your words to bring out the best in others!

THOUGHT OF THE DAY

How can you bring out the best in someone today?

PRAY TODAY

Dear God, I'm so thankful You love me and want me to be my best. Help me to bring out the best in others too! Amen.

A CHEERFUL HEART

A cheerful heart is good medicine, but a broken spirit saps a person's strength.

PROVERBS 17:22 NLT

You may not be a doctor or a nurse, but you can still help a sick friend feel better. How? You can draw a picture for them, send them a card, connect with them on the phone or computer, or pray for God to help them get well. These are all ways to spread some cheer—and the Bible says that "a cheerful heart is good medicine"! And even if their body is OK, a friend might feel sad or lonely. Your cheerful heart can help them feel better too!

THOUGHT OF THE DAY

What is one way you can cheer up someone today?

PRAY TODAY

Dear God, please show me ways I can help others feel better by having a cheerful heart. Amen.

SAYING THE RIGHT THING

How wonderful it is to be able to say the right thing at the right time!

PROVERBS 15:23B TLB

When Laura was sad about being sick on her birthday, Junior told her they could celebrate when she was better. When Larry dropped his tuba and broke it, Bob said he'd help him fix it. Good friends watch and listen, so they know the right words to say. You can do that today! When you pay attention to your friends and understand what they need or want, it's easier to choose your words. Ask God to help you be a good listener, so you can say the right thing at the right time!

THOUGHT OF THE DAY

When you listen to others throughout day, it's easy to know the right thing to say!

PRAY TODAY

Dear Jesus, thank You for always listening to me. Help me listen to others so I can say the right thing at the right time. Amen.

DON'T WORRY

"You keep him in perfect peace whose mind is stayed on you, because he trusts in you."

ISAIAH 26:3 ESV

Do you ever worry? Is it ever hard to fall asleep because you worry about shadows on the walls or strange noises? Maybe you worry if friends will play with you, or if you will do well at school. Our Bible verse says that we can feel peaceful if we choose to think about God and trust in Him. The next time you start to worry, try thinking about how much God loves you. Think about how God is more powerful than anything you are worried about and how He promises He'll always be with you. Then tell your worries to get lost!

THOUGHT OF THE DAY

What worries will you give to God today?

PRAY TODAY

Dear God, I'm so glad that You are greater than anything I worry about. Help me to trust You more. Amen.

GOD LOVES YOUR LAUGH

"He will yet fill your mouth with laughter and your lips with shouts of joy."

JOB 8:21 NIV

The Veggies love to laugh. They make up silly songs and sing them to their friends. They have goofy adventures and share goofy jokes. Did you know that the Bible says God loves for His children to be happy, to laugh, and to be joyful? God has filled the world with things that bring us joy—trees with leaves that dance in the wind, puppies that wrestle and run, kittens that pounce and play. What kinds of things make you laugh? Don't be afraid to giggle, be silly, or sing for joy. God loves to hear you laugh.

THOUGHT OF THE DAY

Do something today that makes you laugh!

PRAY TODAY

Thank You, God, for caring about me and wanting me to laugh and be joyful. Amen.

COURAGE WHEN YOU FEEL AFRAID

Wait for the LORD; be strong, and let your heart take courage.

PSALM 27:14A ESV

Do you think heroes ever feel afraid? They do! Just look in the Bible. Esther risked her life to save her family, but she spent three whole days praying for help first. Barak was a great soldier, but he only agreed to fight a big battle if his friend Deborah came along. Even Jesus felt scared before He was arrested! Real courage means doing the right thing, even when you feel afraid. What's hard for you to feel brave about? God doesn't expect you to do hard things alone. Ask Him for help, then trust Him to give you the courage you need.

THOUGHT OF THE DAY

Next time you feel nervous, stop, pray, and trust. You can be a hero too!

PRAY TODAY

Dear God, when I feel scared, I want to run and hide. Help me stop and pray for courage instead. Amen.

EVERYONE NEEDS FORGIVENESS

Make allowance for each other's faults, and forgive anyone who offends you. Remember, the Lord forgave you, so you must forgive others.

COLOSSIANS 3:13 NLT

Is it ever hard to forgive someone? If you're angry or hurt, it can feel impossible! So the Bible reminds you of something that can help: You've needed forgiveness too.

The next time someone makes you angry, try to remember a time when you made a mistake. Nobody's perfect! That doesn't mean that what happened is OK. But remembering when you've messed up can help you understand that person a little better and maybe feel a little less angry. Talk about how you're feeling. Then ask God to help you forgive. He forgives each of us over and over, so we can do it too!

THOUGHT OF THE DAY

Understanding how someone feels is called empathy.

PRAY TODAY

Dear God, when I get angry, help me remember how many times You've forgiven me. Then help me give that gift to others. Amen.

NEVER ALONE

"Be sure of this—that I am with you always, even to the end of the world."

MATTHEW 28:20B TLB

Just before He returned to heaven, Jesus made a promise to His friends. He said, "I am with you always." It's a promise for you too! When you are feeling alone or lonely, you can remember that Jesus is always with you. An easy way to remember this is to hold up one of your hands, then touch each of your fingers with your other hand. As you touch each finger, say the five words in this verse: I—am—with—you—always. Then put your hand over your heart to remind you that Jesus is there.

THOUGHT OF THE DAY

You are never alone because Jesus is always with you.

PRAY TODAY

Thank You, Jesus, for loving me and always being with me. Amen.

KNOW AND GROW

So faith comes from hearing, that is, hearing the Good News about Christ.

ROMANS 10:17 NLT

Faith is believing and trusting in someone or something. When the Bible talks about having faith in Jesus, it means that you can believe in and trust Him. But you can't have faith in Jesus if you don't know anything about Him. That's why it's important to read and hear the stories and words of Jesus from the Bible. The more you learn about Him, the more your faith will grow. You can memorize Bible verses, learn songs about Jesus, read about Him, and pray to Him. The more you know, the more your faith will grow!

THOUGHT OF THE DAY

What is something you can do today to help your faith grow?

PRAY TODAY

Dear Jesus, thank You for the Bible. Help me learn more about You, so my faith can grow! Amen.

ALWAYS WITH YOU

"The eyes of the LORD watch over those who do right, and his ears are open to their prayers."

1 PETER 3:12A NLT

Do you know that you are never alone? Even when your family can't be with you. Even when your best friend isn't there. Even when you might feel like you are all alone, there is Someone right beside you. You are never alone because Jesus is always there.

The Bible says that Jesus sees what is going on. He knows what you are going through. He loves you and always hears your prayers. So, the next time you feel lonely or like no one understands, remember this promise: You always have a Friend with you. Jesus sees and hears you!

THOUGHT OF THE DAY

How can Jesus help you when you feel alone?

PRAY TODAY

Dear God, thank You for Your promise to always see and hear me. Please help me remember that I am never alone. Amen.

GROWING AND CHANGING

There is a time for everything, and a season for every activity under the heavens.

ECCLESIASTES 3:1 NIV

Sometimes Junior Asparagus wishes everything could stay the same. He likes what he's doing, he likes where he lives, and he likes how old he is! But have you noticed that everything in the world changes? The sun comes up and it goes down, the seasons change, it's lovely one day and stormy the next. You are changing too. You're getting taller, you're learning to do more things, your family needs you to help out more. Change is sometimes hard, but it is also good. It means you are growing. You are becoming the person God created you to be!

THOUGHT OF THE DAY

What are some ways you have changed since your last birthday?

PRAY TODAY

Dear God, thank You for helping me grow. Please help me become the person You want me to be. Amen.

YOUR GOD STORY

All who worship God, come here and listen; I will tell you everything God has done for me.

PSALM 66:16 CEV

Do you love learning about interesting people? Well, guess what? You're one of them!

God made you to be totally unique. And because of that, the way He works in your life is unique too! Does He help you feel confident on your way to school, or calm during arguments? Has He helped you feel better when something sad happened, or brave when you tried something new? Ask God to help you notice His help each day. Those moments make up your very own God story. And it's a great one!

THOUGHT OF THE DAY

Next time someone asks you about God, just tell your story!

PRAY TODAY

Dear God, please help me notice all the ways You show up every day. Let's write a great story together! Amen.

DAY 225

LOOK STRAIGHT AHEAD

Let your eyes look straight ahead; fix your gaze directly before you.

PROVERBS 4:25 NIV

Imagine you're running in a race. You're having a great time! Then suddenly, you start to worry. Where's everyone else? Are they faster than I am? Am I winning? So you turn and look. Sure enough, you find the other runners, but looking around makes you swerve and slow down—maybe even trip and fall! If you had kept your eyes straight ahead, you would have run a better race.

Your life is like that race. God has wonderful plans for each of us. Don't spend time worrying that someone else will be better at one thing or another. Instead trust God to lead you, and keep your eyes on Him!

THOUGHT OF THE DAY

When you're looking at God, you're going the right way!

PRAY TODAY

Dear God, thank You for making a path for me. Please help me when I compare myself with other people. Amen.

DAY 226

GOD IS WITH YOU

The LORD is my light and my salvation; Whom shall I fear? The LORD is the strength of my life; Of whom shall I be afraid?

PSALM 27:1 NKJV

The Bible says we never need to be afraid, because God is always with us. But what if you feel scared anyway? Try remembering today's verse.

First, God is your light. If you're feeling confused, imagine God with a giant flashlight. Trust Him, and He'll help you find the right way! Second, God is your salvation. That means no matter what, you always have a home with God. And third, He's your strength. God can help you do big things because He is stronger than any worries. With God by your side, there's nothing to be afraid of.

THOUGHT OF THE DAY

Fears and worries, go away! God is with me every day.

PRAY TODAY

Dear God, when I feel worried or afraid, please remind me that You are near. Amen.

BE PATIENT AND KIND

Love is patient and kind.

1 CORINTHIANS 13:4A CEV

God knows that we don't always do everything right the first time. But He is patient with us! He forgives us when we make mistakes, and He helps us try again. That's because He loves us. In the Bible He reminds us that we should also show love to others by being patient and kind. When you don't get your way, or when lunch isn't ready when you want it, or when a friend doesn't play just the way you wanted, you can show love by being patient and kind. Things always go better when we remember to be patient and kind.

THOUGHT OF THE DAY

Can you think of a time someone was patient and kind to you? How did it feel?

PRAY TODAY

Dear God, I'm so glad You love me. Please help me be patient and kind, just like You. Amen.

BE JOYFUL!

So rejoice in the LORD and be glad, all you who obey him! Shout for joy, all you whose hearts are pure!

PSALM 32:11 NLT

God loves His children to be joyful! All through the Bible there are stories of people who sang songs to God, danced for God, even clapped and shouted for joy to God! When we think about all the amazing things God has done, it makes us glad. When we do what God says, we learn that He knows the best way for us and we're grateful. When we see His creativity in the world He made, we feel amazed. We are God's children, and He loves us. There are so many reasons to rejoice!

THOUGHT OF THE DAY

What are three things that make you joyful today?

PRAY TODAY

Dear God, thank You for loving me so much. Please help me find reasons to be joyful each day. Amen.

CALL THE DOCTOR!

Be happy with those who are happy. Be sad with those who are sad. Live together in peace with each other.

ROMANS 12:15-16A ICB

You probably know that you feel better when you're cheerful. But did you know that you can share your cheer to help others feel better too? You'll be like a happiness doctor!

Share a hug or a high five with a good friend. Wave to your neighbors when they walk by your house. Invite a new friend to play your favorite game at recess. Tell jokes around the dinner table and see who laughs the hardest! When you have a cheerful heart, share it with the world.

THOUGHT OF THE DAY

Surprise someone who is sad with super silly smiles!

PRAY TODAY

Dear God, I love feeling cheerful! Help me share my smiles with everyone around me! Amen.

FIND WHAT'S GOOD

A happy heart makes the face cheerful, but heartache crushes the spirit.

PROVERBS 15:13 NIV

Some days you just feel grumpy. Here's a game to help your heart feel happy again.

Every time something makes you grumpy, see if you can find something good too. Are you out of your favorite breakfast food? Make something wacky for breakfast instead. Is your friend playing with someone else at recess? Find someone new to play with! Does a rainstorm mean you can't play baseball today? Maybe, but it also means you can play hide-and-seek inside! Spend your time looking for good things, and you'll cheer up your grumpy heart in no time!

THOUGHT OF THE DAY

Look for good things in the bad. Soon you might not feel so sad!

PRAY TODAY

Dear God, when I feel down, please help me find good things to cheer up my heart. Amen.

THE ONLY YOU

For we are God's masterpiece. He has created us anew in Christ Jesus, so we can do the good things he planned for us long ago.

EPHESIANS 2:10 NLT

Do you have a friend who can run super fast? Or a sibling who can draw anything? Or a classmate who always seems to get the right answer? It's tempting to compare yourself with others, especially when they can do something you'd like to be able to do. But God never does that. He made everyone with a unique purpose. That means there is only one you!

If you feel discouraged, remember how much God loves you. Then pray for Him to show you what strengths He's given you. You aren't supposed to be like everyone else. We already have them—the world needs YOU!

THOUGHT OF THE DAY

What are you good at?

PRAY TODAY

Dear God, thank You for making me just the way I am. Please show me how to be the best me! Amen.

LOVE CAN HELP

Hatred stirs up trouble, but love forgives all wrongs.

PROVERBS 10:12 NCV

When someone makes you mad, you might want to stay angry—or even hurt them back! But God tells us to forgive instead.

But how do you do that? The secret is love. Even if you don't feel love for that person yet (it's hard when you're hurt!), look for ways to act lovingly toward them. One way you can do that is to pray for the person who hurt you. Then pick one nice thing to say to them. Choosing not to say unkind words is a loving choice too! The more you practice love, the easier it will be to forgive—this time and every time!

THOUGHT OF THE DAY

How will you choose love next time someone upsets you?

PRAY TODAY

Dear God, will You please help me be loving and forgiving? It sounds a lot better than staying mad. Amen.

A SPECIAL UNIFORM

So, chosen by God for this new life of love, dress in the wardrobe God picked out for you: compassion, kindness, humility, quiet strength, discipline.

COLOSSIANS 3:12 MSG

Some people wear uniforms that help them do their jobs well. Firefighters' special suits keep them safe in burning buildings. Soccer players wear matching jerseys so they can easily spot their teammates. Men and women in the military wear uniforms that tell people about the work they do.

You have important work to do for God. So be sure you're dressed for it! Think about kindness and humility like a jacket you put on every day, or self-control like a favorite hat. Don't leave home without God's special uniform!

THOUGHT OF THE DAY

Dress up in the love of God!

PRAY TODAY

Dear God, when I get up each morning, please help me remember to put on kindness, strength, and self-control too. Amen.

TWO IMPORTANT RULES

Practice God's law—get a reputation for wisdom.

PROVERBS 28:7A MSG

Have you noticed that the world is full of laws or rules? Stop at the stop sign. Don't ride your bike in the street. Don't interrupt when someone else is talking. Stay in your seat at the restaurant. There are so many rules, sometimes it's hard to remember them all!

God wants us to follow His rules too, but His rules are easier to remember. Jesus says there are two important rules that we should always follow: Love God and love other people. If we try to follow those two rules, the Bible says we will be known as wise!

THOUGHT OF THE DAY

What are the two important rules Jesus wants us to remember?

PRAY TODAY

Dear Jesus, I'm so glad You love me. Please help me to always remember to love You and to love other people. Amen.

TAKE YOUR TIME

Enthusiasm without knowledge is not good. If you act too quickly, you might make a mistake.

PROVERBS 19:2 NCV

When you're really excited about something, it's hard to slow down. If you get a new toy, you probably want to use it right away. But if you don't figure out how it works first, you might break it or lose a piece! If your teacher sets out art supplies and you grab them without listening to directions, you could make a mess and spoil your project. Even though it's hard to wait, taking time to think, learn, and follow directions can keep you from making mistakes. And it usually leads to a lot more fun!

THOUGHT OF THE DAY

Can you think of a time when you acted too quickly and made a mistake? What could you do differently next time?

PRAY TODAY

Dear God, please help me to take my time to do things well, to listen, and to follow directions. Amen.

DO THE HARD THING

Don't repay evil for evil. Don't retaliate with insults when people insult you. Instead, pay them back with a blessing.

1 PETER 3:9A NLT

It's normal to want to be mean to someone who is mean to us. But Jesus says that's not a good way to live. It only makes anger and hurting go on and on and on. Instead, Jesus asks us to do a hard thing—to be kind to those who aren't kind to us and to refuse to be mean when someone else is mean. When you are kind and forgiving, you show that you care about Jesus and that you care about others. And it stops meanness right in its tracks! It isn't easy, but it is the best way to live.

THOUGHT OF THE DAY

Who will you choose to be kind to today?

PRAY TODAY

Dear Jesus, You always choose to love everyone. Please help me love others, even when it's hard. Amen.

BUILDING FRIENDSHIPS

Love each other with genuine affection, and take delight in honoring each other.

ROMANS 12:10 NLT

Doesn't it feel great when someone does something nice for you? Maybe they help you solve a problem, let you go first, or give you a compliment. Good friends look for ways to cheer each other on too. Friendships grow stronger when we choose to love and celebrate one another. The next time you're playing or working with a friend, try pointing out something you admire about them. Giving honest support and encouragement makes good friendships even stronger.

THOUGHT OF THE DAY

Who will you encourage today? How will you do that?

PRAY TODAY

Dear God, thank You for my friends. Help me to look for ways to make my friendships even stronger. Amen.

GROWING IN GOD

But grow in the grace and knowledge of our Lord and Savior Jesus Christ. To Him be the glory both now and forever. Amen.

2 PETER 3:18 NKJV

Your body grows bigger and stronger each day. But you can grow in another important way too: You can grow in God!

You grow in your knowledge of God when you read Bible stories and ask good questions. You grow in God's grace when you make choices that show you trust Him. That can mean inviting someone new to play, giving away some of your allowance to help others, or praying when you feel afraid. What's your favorite way to "grow in God"?

THOUGHT OF THE DAY

When you grow strong in God, you can do great things!

PRAY TODAY

Dear God, please help me learn more about You and to trust You more each day. Amen.

COUNT YOUR BLESSINGS

You are wonderful . . . you store up blessings for all who honor and trust you.

PSALM 31:19 CEV

There is an old song that says when you count your blessings, you'll see all that God has done. It's important to remember that every good thing you have is a blessing or gift from God. Blessings can be small like a tiny flower, or huge like the ocean. They can be close, like your family, or far away, like the stars and moon. When you take time to name the good things God has given you, it makes you realize how much He loves you. And it makes you thankful too!

THOUGHT OF THE DAY

How many blessings can you count in one minute?

PRAY TODAY

Dear God, You have given me so many wonderful blessings. Please help me remember to always be thankful to You! Amen.

BE A HELPER

Don't get tired of helping others. You will be rewarded when the time is right, if you don't give up.

GALATIANS 6:9 CEV

Doesn't it make you happy when you have a job to do and a friend offers to help? Maybe you have to walk the dog and your sister comes with you. Maybe you're trying to learn something new, and your buddy helps you practice. When a friend gives you a hand, things are more fun and the work goes faster. So be sure you find ways to help others too! Everyone can use a helping hand, and God even promises to bless us when we take time to help others!

THOUGHT OF THE DAY

Who has helped you recently? Who can you help today?

PRAY TODAY

Dear God, thank You for always helping me. Please show me how I can help someone today. Amen.

SHOW SOME RESPECT

Show respect for all people.

1 PETER 2:17A ICB

Each person in the world is created and loved by God. That's why He tells us in the Bible to "show respect for all people." We show respect when we listen patiently, when we take turns, and when we are kind. We speak with respect when we say *please*, *thanks*, and *I'm sorry*. It is easy to show respect to our best friends, but the Bible says we should show respect for everyone. Practice treating everyone with respect, the way you would like them to treat you, and it will become easier every day.

THOUGHT OF THE DAY

Why do you think God wants us to be respectful to everyone, not just people we like?

PRAY TODAY

Dear God, thank You for creating and loving each person in the world. Help me to show respect to everyone I meet. Amen.

SINGING TO GOD

It is good to praise the Lord and make music to your name, O Most High.

PSALM 92:1 NIV

The world is filled with many different kinds of music. In the city you might hear the rumble of cars, the chimes of a church bell, or the high wail of a fire truck. At the ocean you might hear the roaring waves and the water swishing on the sand. In the woods you might hear birds chirping or frogs croaking.

There are sounds all around you, but the Bible says God especially loves to hear His children making music and singing songs to Him. What kinds of songs can you sing to tell God how much you love Him?

THOUGHT OF THE DAY

What is your favorite kind of music?

PRAY TODAY

Dear God, thank You for giving me a voice so I can sing praises to You! Amen.

WHAT MAKES YOU HAPPY?

I will be happy because of you; God Most High, I will sing praises to your name.

PSALM 9:2 NCV

What makes you happy? Is it getting a new toy or winning a game? These are fun things, but when our happiness depends on what we get, it can quickly disappear when things don't go our way.

The Bible shows us a better way to be happy. We can be happy because of God! Just think about the wonderful things God gives you: God's love lasts forever. He always cares for you, and He will never leave you. Thinking about these things will help you be happy . . . even when you don't get everything you want!

THOUGHT OF THE DAY

Name something God has given you that makes you happy!

PRAY TODAY

Dear God, thinking about how much You love me makes me happy! Thank You! Amen.

GIANT COURAGE

"Don't worry about this Philistine," David told Saul. "I'll go fight him!"

1 SAMUEL 17:32 NLT

David was a young shepherd boy who fought a huge giant named Goliath. It was a scary thing to do, but David trusted God to help Him. David knew that God is bigger than any giant—and that made him feel brave!

Are you doing something scary? Maybe you're moving to a new town, trying a new sport, performing for lots of people, or saying sorry. It's normal to feel afraid sometimes. Just don't let it stop you from doing important things. Remember that God is bigger than anything, and then ask Him to give you courage.

THOUGHT OF THE DAY

Can you think of a time you chose to be brave?

PRAY TODAY

Dear God, sometimes my fear feels taller than a giant. Please remind me that You are even bigger, so I can feel brave! Amen.

HELP YOURSELF

A kind person is doing himself a favor.

PROVERBS 11:17A ICB

Who do you help when you do your chores without complaining? Or write a thank-you note to Grandma? Or invite a new classmate to play with you? You may think you're helping your parents, your grandma, and the new kid. But you're also helping yourself!

Every time you make a kind choice, God blesses you with peace and joy. It's true! God created us to feel warm and happy when we act or speak kindly. Just give it a try! Once you start being kind, you might never want to stop.

THOUGHT OF THE DAY

Try doing something kind for someone right now. How does it feel?

PRAY TODAY

Dear God, please show me ways I can be kind every day! Amen.

GOD CHOSE YOU

Long ago, even before he made the world, God chose us to be his very own through what Christ would do for us. . . . And he did this because he wanted to!

EPHESIANS 1:4–5 TLB

Do you know that long before you were born, even before God created the world, God loved you and chose you to be His very own? You might wonder how this could be! But God is greater than time or space, and He is not limited by what we can understand. He does not love you because of how you look or what you do or even how smart you are. He loves you because He wants to. You are very precious to God. He has always loved you, and He always will! God's love is never-ending!

THOUGHT OF THE DAY

God chose you, and He loves you too. He did this because He wanted to!

PRAY TODAY

Dear God, thank You for loving me with a never-ending love. I am so glad You chose me to be Your very own. Amen.

YOU ARE IMPORTANT

You are young, but do not let anyone treat you as if you were not important. Be an example to show the believers how they should live. Show them with your words, with the way you live, with your love, with your faith, and with your pure life.

1 TIMOTHY 4:12 ICB

Have you ever felt like you aren't important because you're just a kid? There are some things that only grown-ups can do, but the Bible says that young people can do very important things too.

How you talk, how you love others, and how you trust God are all important. With your words you can encourage someone who feels left out. You can share and take turns. You can help someone learn something and listen to what they have to say. These are all ways to care about others. And caring is a very important thing to do!

THOUGHT OF THE DAY

What are some important things you can do today?

PRAY TODAY

Dear God, thank You for loving me and telling me that I am important. Please show me how to share Your love with someone today. Amen.

WHAT IS PRAYER?

I cried to him for help; I praised him with songs.

PSALM 66:17 GNT

Prayer is talking to God. And you can talk to God about anything. You can tell Him about the things that make you happy or sad, excited or mad. You can talk to Him in church or at home, inside or outside. You can say prayers you have memorized or make up your own prayers. You can pray out loud or in your mind, with other people or when you are alone. You can ask God for help or tell Him what you are thankful for. You can even complain to God! God loves you and is always ready to listen.

THOUGHT OF THE DAY

What are some things you want to talk to God about today?

PRAY TODAY

Dear God, thank You for always being there to listen to me when I pray. Please help me to talk with You every day. Amen.

SHOWERS OF BLESSINGS

I said to myself, "Relax and rest. God has showered you with blessings."

PSALM 116:7 MSG

You have probably taken lots of showers. Maybe you've even been caught in a rain shower and gotten totally soaked! But have you ever thought about being showered with blessings?

King David tells us that God gives us so many blessings that it is like being soaked in His love! He gives you help when you need it, a world filled with beautiful things like flowers and forests, pets and friends to play with, a home to live in, and a family that takes care of you. Because God loves you, He showers you with blessings!

THOUGHT OF THE DAY

God showers me with blessings every day, to show that He loves me in every way!

PRAY TODAY

Dear God, thank You so much for all the ways You show me Your love by showering me with blessings. Amen.

SHARE A LITTLE

And God will generously provide all you need. Then you will always have everything you need and plenty left over to share with others.

2 CORINTHIANS 9:8 NLT

You know it's kind to share. Everyone says so! But knowing something is right doesn't make it easier to do. So if sharing is hard for you, here's a trick: start small.

Go through your toys and clothes and find things you can't wear or never play with anymore. Give them to a younger sibling, or ask a grown-up to help you donate them. Bring an extra snack to school in case someone forgot theirs. Let a friend go before you on the swings. Once you get used to sharing a little, you'll see that God always provides for you. Then sharing more will get easier—and more fun!

THOUGHT OF THE DAY

Find one thing you can share with someone today.

PRAY TODAY

Dear God, it's hard to share! Help me share a little today so I can learn to trust You more. Amen.

GOD'S PEACE

And the peace of God, which surpasses every thought, will guard your hearts and minds in Christ Jesus.

PHILIPPIANS 4:7 HCSB

When countries want to end a war, they may sign a peace treaty. The treaty says they will not fight anymore. But sometimes one country breaks the peace treaty, and then they start fighting again. Then peace is gone.

God says He gives His children a different kind of peace. His kind of peace is in your heart. It helps you to stay calm and feel safe even when things around you might not be going well. You can ask God for His peace whenever you feel worried or scared or upset. God's peace is always there for you.

THOUGHT OF THE DAY

When would you want to ask God for His peace?

PRAY TODAY

Dear God, please help me to ask for Your peace whenever I feel worried or afraid. Amen.

BE A FORGIVER

"Rebuke your brother if he sins, and forgive him if he is sorry. Even if he wrongs you seven times a day and each time turns again and asks forgiveness, forgive him."

LUKE 17:3B-4 TLB

Forgiving someone means that we don't try to get even or pay them back. It is not easy. But God says that forgiving is the right thing to do.

God forgives us when we do something wrong. And aren't you glad that He keeps on forgiving even when we make the same mistakes over and over? He wants us to be those kinds of forgivers too! If someone breaks your toy or ruins your project and then says they are sorry, God wants you to be a forgiver. Ask Him to help you when it is hard to forgive.

THOUGHT OF THE DAY

How does it feel when someone forgives you? When will you be a forgiver?

PRAY TODAY

Dear God, I am so glad You always forgive me. Please help me be a forgiver too. Amen.

A BEAUTIFUL HEART

"The mouth speaks the things that are in the heart."

MATTHEW 12:34B ICB

Here's an easy science experiment. Fill a jar with dirty water. Now pour it out. Was the water you poured out clean? Of course not! If you pour dirty water in, you'll get dirty water out!

The same kind of thing can happen in our hearts. If we fill our hearts and minds with things that aren't very nice, then the things we say and do won't be very nice either. But the opposite is true too! Notice and enjoy the good things around you. Read Bible stories that remind you of Jesus and His love. Then your words and actions will reflect the beauty in your heart!

THOUGHT OF THE DAY

How can you fill up on good things?

PRAY TODAY

Dear God, please fill my heart with Your love so the things I say and do will be beautiful! Amen.

BE GLAD TODAY

This is the day that the Lord has made. Let us rejoice and be glad today!

PSALM 118:24 NCV

We all have bad days. Maybe a playdate got cancelled, or you got in trouble—or maybe you just feel grumpy and you're not sure why! If you want to feel better on a bad day, try a little game. Remember that God makes good things, and He made every single day. So try to figure out what might be good about today. It might take some searching, but once you find something, thank God for it—no matter how small! Then, search for something else. Pretty soon, you'll be out of the dumps and praising God!

THOUGHT OF THE DAY

God makes good things every day. Find one that makes you say, "Hooray!"

PRAY TODAY

Dear God, there's always a reason to praise You! On hard days, please help me find a few. Amen.

PICK ONE THING

What joy for those whose strength comes from the LORD.

PSALM 84:5A NLT

Have you ever woken up grumpy? On days like that, it's easy to stay in a bad mood all day. But that's no fun for anyone.

God wants you to feel His joy, even on grumpy days. So try starting small. Pick one thing that makes you happy. Did you eat something yummy for breakfast? Was your favorite shirt clean this morning? Did your pet do something silly? Once you pick something to be happy about, enjoy it! You might even find a few more things to be happy about along the way. God's joy is always ready for you!

THOUGHT OF THE DAY

Ask God to surprise you with joy each day!

PRAY TODAY

Dear God, some days I don't even feel like smiling. Please help me search for Your joy all the time. Amen.

YOU ARE POWERFUL

For the Kingdom of God is not just a lot of talk; it is living by God's power.

1 CORINTHIANS 4:20 NLT

Have you ever wanted a superpower? God gives each of His children an amazing power that they can use every day: the power to bring His kingdom to earth!

You do that by choosing actions that make God happy. Share the things you have. Invite someone new to play. Stand up for yourself and others. Take care of the earth. Tell the truth, even when it's tempting to lie. These things aren't always easy, so ask God to share His power with you. With His help, you can transform your home, your school, and your neighborhood into the kingdom of God!

THOUGHT OF THE DAY

Small actions add up to superpower!

PRAY TODAY

Dear God, You are super awesome! Please help me make kind, wise choices so I can make the world look more like heaven. Amen.

THE GREATEST TEACHER

"I have given you an example to follow. Do as I have done to you."

JOHN 13:15 NLT

Do you have a teacher you love? Great teachers care about their students, help them discover new ideas, and encourage them when they make mistakes or try new things. And do you know the best teacher of all? Jesus!

Jesus loves to help His children grow. He told stories that made people think in new ways. He showed us how to love others and make good choices (even when it's hard). He promises to love you no matter what, and to help you try again when you mess up. With Jesus, there is always more to learn and more to love!

THOUGHT OF THE DAY

When you don't know what to do, check with Jesus—He'll help you!

PRAY TODAY

Dear Jesus, thank You for being the best teacher ever! Amen.

GENTLE WORDS

Be gentle to everyone, able to teach, and patient.

2 TIMOTHY 2:24B HCSB

You probably know that you need to use gentle hands when you touch something that is precious or breakable. But did you ever think about how you also need to be gentle with people's feelings? Words like, "You can't be my friend!" or "I don't like you!" or "You can't play with us!" can hurt people. Gentle words like, "Hi, what's your name?" "Would you like a turn?" and "You can sit by me" help others feel wanted. Gentle words help instead of hurt. It's important to think about how your words make others feel. Practice using gentle words.

THOUGHT OF THE DAY

How can you use gentle words today?

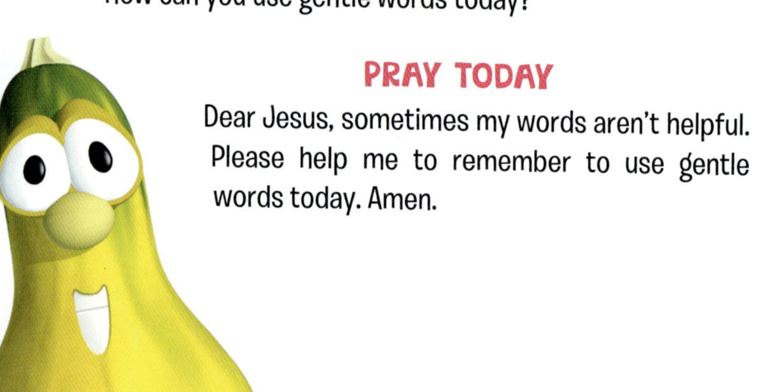

PRAY TODAY

Dear Jesus, sometimes my words aren't helpful. Please help me to remember to use gentle words today. Amen.

TRUE FRIEND

"And you are my friends, if you obey me. Servants don't know what their master is doing, and so I don't speak to you as my servants. I speak to you as my friends, and I have told you everything my Father has told me."

JOHN 15:14-15 CEV

One of the special things about having a best friend (or a few!) is that you can tell each other everything. You can share what you're excited about and what you're worried about. You can ask for help and share ideas. You can be yourself and know that your friend understands—even when you make mistakes! Best friends learn to trust and love each other. Did you know that Jesus wants to be that kind of friend to you? He loves you, and He wants you to love Him too. Will you talk to Him and listen to Him today?

THOUGHT OF THE DAY

When you read Jesus' words in the Bible, you're reading a letter from your best Friend!

PRAY TODAY

Dear Jesus, thank You for being my very best Friend and for always listening whenever I talk to You. Amen.

CLEAN ON THE INSIDE

Create in me a pure heart, God, and make my spirit right again.

PSALM 51:10 NCV

When you get dirty playing in the mud, you can take a bath to get clean again. If you get some ketchup on your shirt, you can wash it. But what can you do if you do something wrong or hurt someone's feelings and you feel icky? How can you get clean on the inside? The Bible says that God can give us clean hearts and make things right again. He knows we make mistakes, and He wants us to feel clean and good. If we ask Him to forgive us and help us, He will!

THOUGHT OF THE DAY

God can change your sad heart to a glad heart! Just ask Him!

PRAY TODAY

Dear God, thank You for loving me and promising to help me have a clean heart! Amen.

REAL WINNERS

Happiness comes to those who are fair to others and are always just and good.

PSALM 106:3 TLB

When someone cheats at a game, refuses to take turns, or teases someone, it may seem like they win, but instead, they really lose. They lose the trust and respect of others. They lose friends because others don't like being treated unfairly. Real winners may not always score the most points or win a game, but they play by the rules and choose to be good sports, no matter who leads on the scoreboard. Real winners help everyone have a good time, and they end up being happier too! Choose to be a real winner—you'll be much happier in the end.

THOUGHT OF THE DAY

What will you do to be a real winner today?

PRAY TODAY

Dear God, please help me to be a real winner—to play fairly and treat everyone with respect. Amen.

FACING FEAR

As Goliath moved closer to attack, David quickly ran out to meet him.

1 SAMUEL 17:48 NLT

David was just a young shepherd boy when he accepted the challenge to fight the giant, Goliath. He was probably scared and nervous. He could have run away. He could have refused. But David knew something that made him brave enough for the battle. He knew that God was on his side, and that God would help him defeat his enemy! And guess what? If you trust in God, He will help you too. He'll help you be brave when you need to do what is right. Just like David, you can face your fears with courage from God!

THOUGHT OF THE DAY

God promises He is always near to help you face the things you fear!

PRAY TODAY

Dear God, thank You for loving me and giving me enough courage to face whatever I'm afraid of. Amen.

ONE PERFECT THING

Let your unfailing love surround us, LORD, for our hope is in you alone.

PSALM 33:22 NLT

Have you ever trusted something that let you down? Maybe a friend hurt your feelings. Or your birthday party got rained on. Maybe you built an amazing fort, only to have it collapse as soon as you got inside! People, weather, and even blanket forts aren't perfect. But God's love is.

When things don't go your way, it's OK to feel disappointed—even angry! Try to remember that God is with you. You can always ask for His help—to mend a friendship, change your plans, and design something new. He'll never fail you.

THOUGHT OF THE DAY

When something doesn't go your way, remember God is here to stay.

PRAY TODAY

Dear God, it's so hard when things go wrong. Please help me find comfort in knowing You always care. Amen.

GOD'S GOOD PLANS

"I know that You can do all things. Nothing can put a stop to Your plans."

JOB 42:2 NLV

We often think about the future—What will happen? Who will be my friend? Will I do well in school or sports? Will we have to move? There are so many things to wonder about.

We can make plans, but sometimes our plans change. That's because we aren't in control of what happens in the future! But here's some great news: God knows all about the future, and He has plans that cannot be changed. God knows what is best, and nothing can stop His good plans! Trust Him when you aren't sure about your future.

THOUGHT OF THE DAY

What things in your future will you trust God to work out for good?

PRAY TODAY

Dear God, I am so glad that You have good plans for my future. Please help me to put my trust in You! Amen.

NEVER LOST

"What man among you, who has 100 sheep and loses one of them, does not leave the 99 in the open field and go after the lost one until he finds it?"

LUKE 15:4 HCSB

Have you ever lost something important? There's nothing you want more than to find it again! When Jesus wanted His friends to understand His great love for them, He used the idea of finding a precious lost treasure.

Jesus will never lose us, but sometimes it feels like we're far away from Him. Are you going through a sad or scary time? Have you made a choice that you know isn't right? You never have to worry. He has not forgotten you. He is always there, ready to welcome you into His loving arms.

THOUGHT OF THE DAY

When you feel lost and all alone, God will always lead you home.

PRAY TODAY

Dear God, I'm so glad You never leave me. Help me remember that when I feel lost. Amen.

FOLLOW JESUS

"My sheep hear My voice, I know them, and they follow Me."

JOHN 10:27 HCSB

Jesus often called Himself a "Shepherd" and His followers "sheep." A shepherd takes good care of his sheep and protects them. He knows their names, and they follow him because they know he loves them.

When Jesus lived on earth, His followers could talk with Him. But today we hear Jesus' words in the Bible. We hear Him say things like, "Love one another." "Be kind." "Help the helpless." If you belong to Jesus, you are one of His sheep too. Read your Bible, listen for His voice, then follow Him!

THOUGHT OF THE DAY

Following Jesus, your Shepherd, means listening to what He has to say!

PRAY TODAY

Dear God, thank You for giving me the words of Jesus in the Bible. Help me to hear His voice every day. Amen.

SAYING WHAT'S TRUE

"These are the things you are to do: Speak the truth to each other."

ZECHARIAH 8:16A NIV

Speaking the truth means saying what really happened. If you take something and break it, when someone asks, "What happened?" you say, "I took it and I broke it." If you run into someone on the playground, you say, "I'm sorry I bumped into you. Are you OK?"

It's sometimes hard to tell the truth if you're afraid you might get into trouble or someone will be disappointed. But when you tell the truth, people know they can trust you. Good friends say what is true—even when it's hard to do.

THOUGHT OF THE DAY

Can you talk about a time when you told the truth?

PRAY TODAY

Dear God, I want to be someone who tells the truth. Please help me, even when it's hard to do. Amen.

WHO IS THE GREATEST TEACHER?

"Teacher, I will follow you wherever you go."

MATTHEW 8:19B ESV

What makes a teacher great? They not only tell you how to do things, but they also show you how to do them. They listen to you, and they help when you don't understand things. Great teachers are caring and patient when you make mistakes. They don't give up on you!

Jesus was that kind of teacher! That's why His disciples and friends wanted to follow Him. He wants to be your teacher too. You can learn how to follow Him by reading your Bible and praying for His help. He's the greatest teacher ever!

THOUGHT OF THE DAY

Who is one of your favorite teachers? Why?

PRAY TODAY

Dear God, I am so glad that You sent Jesus to teach me how to live. Please help me to follow and learn from Him every day. Amen.

CHASING AWAY WORRIES

Worry is a heavy burden, but a kind word always brings cheer.

PROVERBS 12:25 CEV

Larry was worried about performing in the talent show. He worried about tripping or bumping into the microphone—or what if he forgot all the words? When Bob saw how worried Larry was, he reminded Larry how everyone loved him and would be cheering for him. Bob's kind words chased away Larry's worries. When you see that a friend is worried, you can help them too! Take time to speak kind and encouraging words to them. Tell them that you believe they can do hard things, and you'll be cheering them on. Kind words can chase away worries!

THOUGHT OF THE DAY

Who needs your help to chase away their worries? What kind words will you say to them?

PRAY TODAY

Dear God, thank You for helping me when I'm worried. Please show me how I can help others when they are worried too. Amen.

A SPECIAL SIGN

"The rainbow that I have put in the sky will be my sign to you and to every living creature on earth."

GENESIS 9:12 CEV

Did you know that there is a special sign in the Bible that you can still see today? When the sun shines through raindrops, you can see a colorful arc of light in the sky. It is called a rainbow. God made the first rainbow as a sign of His loving promise to Noah's family. That first rainbow appeared thousands of years ago. And we can still see rainbows today. Whenever you see a rainbow, remember how much God loved Noah and how much He loves you too!

THOUGHT OF THE DAY

Draw a rainbow and put it in your room to remind you of God's love.

PRAY TODAY

Dear God, thank You for giving me beautiful rainbows to remind me of Your love. Amen.

NOTHING IS IMPOSSIBLE FOR GOD

Jesus looked at them intently, then said, "Without God, it is utterly impossible. But with God everything is possible."

MARK 10:27 TLB

Many things Jesus taught His friends seemed impossible to them. He said they should love their enemies and trust God when they were in danger. He told them to be kind to people who were mean to them. When they said, "How can we do these things?" Jesus told them, "With God everything is possible." Sometimes you will face things that seem impossible—you might be afraid of the dark, or have a fight with a friend, or make a big mistake. You can trust God to help you when things seem impossible. He is always there for you!

THOUGHT OF THE DAY

What is something that seems impossible for you? Will you trust God to help you?

PRAY TODAY

Dear God, I am so glad that nothing is impossible for You! Please help me to trust You to help me when things seem too hard for me. Amen.

A WONDERFUL BODY

I will praise You because I have been remarkably and wonderfully made. Your works are wonderful, and I know this very well.

PSALM 139:14 HCSB

Did you know that every minute your heart beats about 100 times and you breathe in and out about 25 times? The most amazing thing is that you never even have to think about it! You don't have to remind your heart to beat. You don't have to remember to breathe.

Didn't God make you a wonderful body? Your heart, lungs, and many other parts keep working on their own so you can focus on things like learning or making friends! So be sure to make healthy choices for your body. It's one way of saying "thank You" to God for this great gift!

THOUGHT OF THE DAY

What are some things you do to take care of your body?

PRAY TODAY

Dear God, thank You for giving me such a wonderful body. Help me to take good care of it every day. Amen.

CELEBRATE DIFFERENCES

We have different gifts, according to the grace given to each of us.

ROMANS 12:6A NIV

The Veggies know that they are each special and they are each good at different things. Larry plays several musical instruments and makes up the silliest songs. Bob the Tomato is a great friend and loves to learn new things. Petunia is known for her kindness, and Pa Grape is filled with wisdom. Just like the Veggies, each person has different likes, dislikes, talents, and interests. That's how God made us! It's important to thank God for our different gifts. They are all wonderful and worth celebrating!

THOUGHT OF THE DAY

What are some things that make you special and different from your friends?

PRAY TODAY

Thank You, God, for making each person special. Help me enjoy and celebrate the differences I see around me. Amen.

BE GENEROUS

Give generously, for your gifts will return to you later.

ECCLESIASTES 11:1 TLB

Being generous means giving more than is expected. Sometimes that means sharing what you have, even if you end up with less.

You might give someone part of your snack when you would prefer to keep it all or spend time helping a friend when you wanted to play by yourself. You could also give away some of your toys, clothes, or books to someone who doesn't have as much. Those are all good ways to be generous! God says that when you're generous, you will receive blessings. Those blessings might be a happy feeling in your heart or might be gifts when you need them too!

THOUGHT OF THE DAY

Name some ways you can be generous today.

PRAY TODAY

Dear God, thank You for always being generous to me and giving me more than I expect. Please help me to be generous to others. Amen.

FINISH THE JOB

"Solomon, you must understand this. The Lord has chosen you to build the Temple as his holy place. Be strong and finish the job."

1 CHRONICLES 28:10 ICB

It is fun to start a project. You have great ideas and are excited to try them out. But after a while, the work sometimes seems hard or boring. You might be tempted to quit. But that's just the time to remember that God has promised to help you be strong! He can help you finish any tough job. Are you learning to dance or to play soccer? Don't give up when things are hard or when you feel like you aren't doing well. Be strong and finish the job. God loves to help you, even when you feel like quitting.

THOUGHT OF THE DAY

What work would you like God to help you finish?

PRAY TODAY

Dear God, I'm glad You give me work to do. Will You please help me finish what I start? Amen.

NO MORE GRUDGES

Be gentle and ready to forgive; never hold grudges. Remember, the Lord forgave you, so you must forgive others. Most of all, let love guide your life.

COLOSSIANS 3:13-14A TLB

Do you know what a grudge is? It is choosing to stay mad at someone because something they said or did made you upset. We all get mad sometimes, and that's OK. But God wants us to be willing to forgive others instead of staying mad at them. He knows that holding grudges only makes us unhappy. God loves us, so He chooses to forgive us. And that's how He wants us to treat others too—it helps everyone feel better (including you!). So the next time you are tempted to hold a grudge, forgive instead. You'll be glad you did!

THOUGHT OF THE DAY

Forgiving is God's way of living!

PRAY TODAY

Dear God, thank You so much for always forgiving me. Help me to let go of grudges and forgive others too! Amen.

DO WHAT'S RIGHT

Now, Israel, listen to the laws and commands I will teach you. Obey them so that you will live.

DEUTERONOMY 4:1A NCV

Making right choices is always good, but sometimes it is hard to do. Maybe your friends are making a poor choice and they want you to do the same thing. What will you do then?

It helps to remember that God loves you and is watching over you. He wants to help you do what is right, even when it's hard. Ask Him to give you courage to make good choices. He promises to surprise you with blessings when you follow Him!

THOUGHT OF THE DAY

When you need to make a choice about doing what is right, always ask God for His help.

PRAY TODAY

Dear God, I'm so glad You love me and want me to do what is right. Help me remember to call on You when I have to make hard choices. Amen.

GOD'S GIFTS

For the LORD God is our sun and our shield. He gives us grace and glory. The LORD will withhold no good thing from those who do what is right.

PSALM 84:11 NLT

Isn't it exciting to get gifts at Christmas and on your birthday? Your friends and family give you gifts because they love you and want you to be happy. But do you know who else loves to give you gifts? God! God gives you sunshine and rain, a body that is growing, friends and family who care about you, and the ability to learn new things. God's gifts don't cost money, but they are more precious than anything you could buy. God gives you gifts because He loves you more than you can imagine.

THOUGHT OF THE DAY

Can you name some of the wonderful gifts God has given you?

PRAY TODAY

Dear God, thank You for giving me so much. Please help me use the gifts You have given me to bless others. Amen.

BE KIND AND FORGIVE

Be kind and compassionate to one another, forgiving each other, just as in Christ God forgave you.

EPHESIANS 4:32 NIV

When someone breaks your toy or hurts your feelings, you probably feel sad or mad. You might even want to get even by breaking something of theirs or saying something hurtful back to them. But that just makes the hurt go on and on. Jesus shows us a better way. He reminds us that He always forgives us. We can copy Jesus by being kind and caring toward others too. We can forgive them. We can refuse to get even or hurt others back. When we forgive, we are showing love, and that makes God happy!

THOUGHT OF THE DAY

The best way to live is to be kind and forgive!

PRAY TODAY

Dear Jesus, thank You for forgiving me when I make mistakes. Please help me to be kind and forgiving toward others. Amen.

THE PERFECT PRESENT

God loves the person who gives happily.

2 CORINTHIANS 9:7B ICB

It's fun to pick out just the right gift for someone you love! You can wrap it in pretty paper and look forward to the moment they'll open it.

But sometimes giving isn't so fun. It's hard to give your time to a sibling who needs help, or to put some of your allowance in the offering plate, or to give a friend your last cookie. But God says that each time we give something away, we should do it cheerfully. So next time you have a chance to share what you have, imagine you're wrapping up a beautiful birthday present. Then hand it over with a smile!

THOUGHT OF THE DAY

Being a cheerful giver takes practice. Look for ways to share what you have each day!

PRAY TODAY

Dear God, please help me share with a smile. It's hard to give things away sometimes, and I could use Your help. Amen.

WAYS TO PRAISE

The LORD is my strength and my song; He has become my salvation. This is my God, and I will praise Him.

EXODUS 15:2A HCSB

The best gift you can give God is your praise. He loves to see you enjoy His world and to hear what makes you happy. You probably know you can praise God when you pray, but did you know you can use your special gifts to praise Him in SO many other ways too?

You can make up a song to say what you're thankful for or create a joyful dance just for Him! Try drawing a picture of something you love. Even asking questions and learning more about the world shows God how much you appreciate His creation. How will you choose to praise God today?

THOUGHT OF THE DAY

Praise God any kind of way. Try to do it every day!

PRAY TODAY

Dear God, You are amazing! I love You and I want to praise You any way I can! Amen.

DAY 282

YOU'RE IMPORTANT TO GOD

God began doing a good work in you, and I am sure he will continue it until it is finished when Jesus Christ comes again.

PHILIPPIANS 1:6 NCV

God has great plans for you. And those plans have already started! God can use everything you learn and experience to help develop your gifts. He brings people into your life who will encourage and support you. He's listening every time you pray, guiding you to make good choices and to learn from your mistakes. He is with you every moment of every day.

Sometimes it feels like nothing goes right. But when that happens, try to remember God's great love. He's doing good work in you, and He'll keep doing it. You are so important to Him!

THOUGHT OF THE DAY

You're a big part of God's plan!

PRAY TODAY

Dear God, it feels good to know I matter so much to You! Thanks for doing good work in me. Amen.

BE AN ENCOURAGER

You must encourage one another each day.

HEBREWS 3:13A CEV

If you are having a hard time or feeling sad, doesn't it feel great when someone comes along and cheers you up? Encouragement is a great gift we can give to each other. Sometimes we give encouragement with words like "I know you can do it" or "Keep on trying" or "I'm on your side." At other times, we don't even have to use words to encourage someone. A hug, a pat on the back, or just sitting with someone can be encouraging. You can find ways to encourage others every day—just give it a try!

THOUGHT OF THE DAY

Who will you encourage today?

PRAY TODAY

Dear Lord, Your loving care always encourages me. Please help me to find ways to encourage someone else today. Amen.

LIVING IN UNITY

How good and how pleasant it is when God's people live together in unity!

PSALM 133:1 NIV

Have you noticed how everyone is different? Some of us are tall and some are short. We have different colored hair and skin. Some of us love sports, while others love art or reading. Some like to be loud, and others prefer quiet. Some of us live in cities, and some live in the country. Even with all these differences, God wants us to live together in unity. Unity means that we care about each other and try hard to understand and learn from one another. When we live in unity, God says it is good for everyone!

THOUGHT OF THE DAY

How are you the same as, and different from, your friends?

PRAY TODAY

Dear God, thank You for our differences. Help me to treat each person I know with the same love You show me. Amen.

TRUST GOD'S PLAN

"I know what I am planning for you," says the LORD. "I have good plans for you, not plans to hurt you. I will give you hope and a good future."

JEREMIAH 29:11 NCV

Thousands of years ago, when God's people faced a fearsome enemy, God gave them a wonderful promise. He said that although things looked scary, He had good plans for them. They could trust Him.

The good news is that God still has good plans for people who trust Him. That means you! Sometimes the future can look scary. What will happen? Who will be your friends? What will you be when you grow up? You don't know the answers to all these questions, but the one big answer is that God has good plans for you! Trust Him!

THOUGHT OF THE DAY

When you're not sure what you should do, you can trust God's plans for you!

PRAY TODAY

Dear God, I am so thankful that You have good plans for me. Please help me to learn to trust You more every day. Amen.

PEACE STARTS AT HOME

You're blessed when you can show people how to cooperate instead of compete or fight.

MATTHEW 5:9A MSG

Families are a gift from God. But it's normal to argue sometimes. What's important is how you work through your disagreements. Next time you feel an argument starting, try the "3 Fs."

Be Friendly: Choose kind words instead of mean ones.

Be Flexible: Look for a solution that works for everyone—not just you.

Be Forgiving: Remember that everyone makes mistakes. Can you be the one who offers forgiveness first?

You won't always agree with everyone in your family. But when you work hard to get along, your home will be loving and peaceful!

THOUGHT OF THE DAY

You can use the 3 Fs with friends and classmates too!

PRAY TODAY

Dear God, help me get along with my family, even when we disagree. I love having a peaceful home! Amen.

YOUR FATHER IN HEAVEN

"Pray like this: Our Father in heaven, may your name be kept holy. May your Kingdom come soon. May your will be done on earth, as it is in heaven."

MATTHEW 6:9-10 NLT

When Jesus' friends asked Him to teach them how to pray, He told them to talk to God as if He were their heavenly Father. A good father loves his children. He wants what is best for them, and he always listens to them. You can talk to your heavenly Father about anything. You can tell Him about what worries you. You can ask Him for help. You can tell Him what you are happy about. And you can pray anywhere at any time. Your heavenly Father is never too busy to listen to you, His beloved child!

THOUGHT OF THE DAY

What are some things you want to say to your heavenly Father?

PRAY TODAY

Dear God, I'm so glad You are my Father in heaven. Thank You for always being there and for always listening to me. Amen.

BE CONSIDERATE

Let everyone see that you are considerate in all you do.

PHILIPPIANS 4:5A NLT

Do you know what it means to be considerate? It means to consider—or think about—others' feelings. If you notice that someone has been left out, you might talk to them and invite them to play with you. If a friend isn't sure how to solve a problem, you could help them think of solutions. If others make fun of someone, you can choose kindness by standing up for them instead. Being considerate means treating others the way you would like to be treated. It's that simple!

THOUGHT OF THE DAY

How can you be considerate at home today?

PRAY TODAY

Dear God, thank You for loving and caring about me. Please help me to be more considerate of others. Amen.

CONTINUE SEEKING GOD

"Continue to ask, and God will give to you. Continue to search, and you will find. Continue to knock, and the door will open for you."

MATTHEW 7:7 ICB

When you are just learning something new, it's easy to get discouraged. Whether you are learning how to sound out words, how to kick a ball, or how to sing a song, it will take many tries to get it right or do it well. But if you don't continue, you may not learn at all! Learning about God also takes practice. When you practice praying, it becomes easier. When you practice trusting God, your faith grows. When you practice doing what God says, you become a stronger believer. Continue seeking God and He promises you will find Him!

THOUGHT OF THE DAY

How will you seek God today?

PRAY TODAY

Dear God, I'm glad You want me to find You. Please help me seek You each day. Amen.

STRONGER THAN TEMPTATION

"Stay awake and pray for strength against temptation. The spirit wants to do what is right, but the body is weak."

MATTHEW 26:41 NCV

Temptation is when you know you shouldn't do something, but you really really want to. Have you ever felt that way? You know what's right, but the wrong choice just looks easier or more fun . . . or both!

God says you need strength to fight against temptation. One way to get stronger is to make a plan! Decide what you'll do next time you feel tempted. Will you ask for help? Will you walk away from the cookie jar or from kids who are teasing someone else? Ask God for ideas. With His strength, temptation won't stand a chance!

THOUGHT OF THE DAY

Even Jesus faced temptation—He can help you be strong too!

PRAY TODAY

Dear God, sometimes it's hard to choose the right thing. Please give me strength when I'm tempted. Amen.

SHARING GROWS!

"If you have two shirts, share with the person who does not have one. If you have food, share that too."

LUKE 3:11B ICB

So many great things happen when you share! First, you are taking care of others. You might have something that someone else really needs and you can bless them by sharing it. Second, you're acting in a loving way. Whenever you do that, you show people a little bit of what God looks like. How cool is that? Third, you might inspire them to share with someone else. That means your kindness could help people you don't even know! And finally, joy, love, and peace will grow in your heart. So get out there and share!

THOUGHT OF THE DAY

Don't be surprised if sharing once makes you want to share even more!

PRAY TODAY

Dear God, thank You for all the ways You've blessed me. Help me share those blessings with others. Amen.

DAY 292

FOCUS ON YOU

God blesses those people who are merciful. They will be treated with mercy!

MATTHEW 5:7 CEV

You can't change the way anyone else acts. But you don't have to. Instead, God wants you to focus on yourself. What can YOU do to help others and show love?

One of the most important things you can do is to be kind to everyone. Even people you don't like. Even when someone is mean to you. Even when your little sister breaks a toy you told her not to touch. Your actions might change the way others behave, or they might not. But choosing kindness every day will change you!

THOUGHT OF THE DAY

God is working on your heart. Trust Him to work on everyone else's too!

PRAY TODAY

Dear God, please help me focus on my own actions instead of anyone else's. Thank You for helping me grow each day! Amen.

EVERYDAY MIRACLES

"God can do anything!"

LUKE 1:37 NCV

Sometimes when we think about the amazing things God does, we imagine Him creating billions of stars, gigantic oceans, or enormous mountains. It is easy to overlook the miracles God does every day. Every tiny seed that sprouts is a miracle! It is a miracle that your body works the way it does. It's a miracle that you can invent and imagine new ideas. It is a miracle when God helps you forgive someone or changes a wrong attitude to be right. Nothing is too big or small for God to do because He can do anything!

THOUGHT OF THE DAY

Name some everyday miracles you see!

PRAY TODAY

Dear God, thank You for creating the world and everything in it. I'm so glad You can do anything! Amen.

CONTROL YOURSELF

Losing self-control leaves you as helpless as a city without a wall.

PROVERBS 25:28 CEV

In Bible times, people built large walls around their cities to keep enemies and wild animals out. A city without a wall was in danger. Today's Bible verse says that a person who loses self-control is also in danger. When you control your temper, you don't say or do things that might hurt yourself or someone else. And when you use self-control and follow the rules at school or in your neighborhood, you keep yourself and others safe. Can you think of some other ways that learning to control yourself will help avoid danger?

THOUGHT OF THE DAY

Make it your goal to show self-control!

PRAY TODAY

Dear Lord, I'm so glad You love me and want me to be safe. Please help me practice self-control. Amen.

FRIENDS FOREVER

Jesus Christ is the same yesterday and today and forever.

HEBREWS 13:8 ESV

Friends are a wonderful gift from God! It's fun to find people who like the same things you do. Some friendships last for years, and some only last a short time. Friends might move away or just decide they like different things. Everyone grows and changes, and that means friendships grow and change too. But one friend will never change: Jesus. He has always loved you, even before you were born. He will always be with you. He will guide you and hear your prayers wherever you go. No matter what happens, you and Jesus will be friends forever!

THOUGHT OF THE DAY

How does it feel to know Jesus is your friend?

PRAY TODAY

Dear Jesus, thank You for being my very best friend forever! Amen.

ALL IN THE FAMILY

His unchanging plan has always been to adopt us into his own family by sending Jesus Christ to die for us. And he did this because he wanted to!

EPHESIANS 1:5 TLB

No two families are the same. But every family is a gift from God! You might not feel that way when you're arguing with your little brother or when your dad gives you extra chores. But the people in your life help you grow into the person God wants you to be. Everyone in a family is important. We have unique gifts and personalities, and we can help each other in different ways.

In fact, family is so important that God sent Jesus so that we could all be part of His family too! With God as our Father, we will always be loved, cherished, and cared for.

THOUGHT OF THE DAY

Find a way to help your family today!

PRAY TODAY

Dear God, I love being in Your family! Thank You for all the ways You care for me. Amen.

IT'S FUN TO BE KIND

Finally, all of you, be like-minded, be sympathetic, love one another, be compassionate and humble.

1 PETER 3:8 NIV

You know that God asks you to be kind. But did you also know that being kind can be fun?

Do you like to draw? Make cards for all your neighbors or help a friend draw something new. Can you read? Read a book to a younger sibling while your mom and dad are making dinner. Is there someone who always sits alone at recess? Invite him or her to play with you. See how fast you can clean up a mess without being asked. Tell someone your favorite thing about them! Be kind any chance you get. Then don't be surprised if others join the fun too!

THOUGHT OF THE DAY

What's your favorite way to be kind?

PRAY TODAY

Dear God, I'm glad there are so many ways to be kind. Help me show everyone how fun it can be! Amen.

GOD IS THERE FOR YOU

"The LORD himself will fight for you. Just stay calm."

EXODUS 14:14 NLT

It's easy to trust God when everything is fun and easy. But what if you're scared? There was a time in the Bible when Moses helped God's people escape from their enemies. But when their enemies chased after them, God's people were terrified! Then Moses reminded them that God was with them, and He would fight for them. They only needed to calm down and trust God.

Do you know that God is always there for you too? When you're facing something that makes you afraid, ask God to help you be calm and trust Him.

THOUGHT OF THE DAY

Whenever you don't know what to do, remember God is there for you!

PRAY TODAY

Dear God, I'm so thankful that You are here for me! Please help me remember to call on You whenever I'm afraid. Amen.

THE BEST LISTENER

I cried to him for help; I praised him with songs.

PSALM 66:17 GNT

At church, you might hear all kinds of prayers. Sometimes people use a lot of fancy words to pray. Other times, they sound like they're talking with a good friend. Prayers can sound sad or joyful or even confused and angry. Sometimes people ask God for things, and sometimes they just tell God how wonderful He is. They might even do both in the same prayer! God listens to each and every kind of prayer.

No matter how you're feeling, you can always talk to God. You don't have to know any special words. God will always listen to you.

THOUGHT OF THE DAY

God loves to hear your prayers. Talk to Him today!

PRAY TODAY

Dear God, thank You for always caring about me and listening to all my prayers. Amen.

LOVE EVERYONE?

"There is a saying, 'Love your friends and hate your enemies.' But I say: Love your enemies! Pray for those who persecute you!"

MATTHEW 5:43-44 TLB

Has anyone ever been mean to you? That feels pretty rotten. Maybe you even thought about being mean to them in return.

But Jesus tells us to do something else: Love and pray for people who are mean to you! That's not just surprising, it's HARD. So ask for God's help. Sometimes people are mean because they are unhappy—try praying for happiness in that person's life. Plan for how you will choose kindness toward them. You don't have to become best friends. But maybe your love and prayers will help them become a little more friendly!

THOUGHT OF THE DAY

Remember that love is an action: You don't have to feel loving to show love to others!

PRAY TODAY

Dear God, will You please show me how to love and pray for everyone, even when they are mean? I need Your help. Amen.

HELP YOUR FRIENDS

We should keep on encouraging each other to be thoughtful and to do helpful things.

HEBREWS 10:24 CEV

Knives need to be sharp to do good work. To sharpen a dull knife, a person scrapes the blade along another piece of metal. The pieces of metal help each other!

You have good work to do too. God needs you to be the best YOU that you can be! So He gives you good friends to help you do just that. Good friends help each other learn new things, be brave, and choose kindness. And the best friends gently remind us when we need to fix something we've done wrong. Friends keep each other "sharp" so they can do great things!

THOUGHT OF THE DAY

Can you help a friend make a good choice today?

PRAY TODAY

Dear God, help me be a friend who helps others—and help me choose friends like that too! Amen.

FEELING SPECIAL

Don't be selfish. . . . Be humble, thinking of others as better than yourself.

PHILIPPIANS 2:3 TLB

Being first makes us feel special! When you're the line leader, when it's your birthday, or when you get to talk in front of the class, you get extra attention. It is great to be first sometimes! And it's important to help others feel special too. Giving a compliment, sharing a toy, and letting someone go ahead of you are all ways to put others first and make them feel special. Try it! It's fun to share that special feeling, and it makes Jesus happy too!

THOUGHT OF THE DAY

Can you think of three ways to make someone else feel special today?

PRAY TODAY

Dear God, I am so glad that You treat me as Your special child. Please help me to find ways to help others know they are special too! Amen.

LEARN TO FORGIVE

Pleasant words are like a honeycomb, making people happy and healthy.

PROVERBS 16:24 NCV

Have you ever done or said something that made someone else feel bad? Has anyone ever hurt your feelings? When that happens, forgiveness helps everyone feel better.

Forgiving someone means you choose not to get even. You decide to be kind instead of being mean or staying angry. Forgiving helps friendships grow stronger. When you forgive, you are doing something that Jesus did! You're learning to be more like Him. There are times when we all need to be forgiven and times when we all need to learn to forgive. Jesus can help you with both!

THOUGHT OF THE DAY

Learn to be kind, to love, and forgive. It's the way Jesus wants us to live!

PRAY TODAY

Dear God, thank You for loving and forgiving me. Please help me to learn to be kind and forgive others. Amen.

FINDING TRUE HAPPINESS

"It is more blessed to give than to receive."

ACTS 20:35B ESV

When you receive a gift, get a special award, or win a prize, it makes you happy. But Jesus told His friends a special way to feel even happier: give to others!

If you take the time to make a gift or card for someone, you feel great when you give it to them. If you help someone with a chore or teach them how to do something, you get a happy feeling because you helped them out. Jesus gave all He had to us, and He knows that when we give to others, we find true happiness!

THOUGHT OF THE DAY

Who will you give something to today?

PRAY TODAY

Dear God, thank You for giving me so much. Please help me to find ways to give to others and find true happiness. Amen.

BE A LIGHT

The light shines in the darkness, and the darkness has not overcome it.

JOHN 1:5 ESV

Have you ever been afraid of the dark? When it is dark you can't see things well. You could trip and fall. Noises or shapes can seem scary. But if you turn on the light, the darkness goes away!

Jesus says that His words and His love can be like a light that is greater than any darkness in the world. When you are kind, helpful, or tell someone that Jesus loves them, you bring God's light to them. They don't have to be afraid of feeling alone or unloved anymore. Be a light to others today!

THOUGHT OF THE DAY

Can you think of three ways to be a light to someone today?

PRAY TODAY

Dear God, I want to be a light today! Show me ways to help others who feel afraid or alone. Amen.

GOD IS ALWAYS WITH YOU

Give all your worries to him, because he cares about you.

1 PETER 5:7 NCV

Do you ever feel lonely? When you go somewhere new, like camp or a new class, and you don't know anyone, it can be a little scary. Maybe you're spending the night away from home, and you feel homesick. Our Bible verse today reminds us that even when your friends or your parents aren't with you, God is always near. He never leaves you. You can talk to Him and ask Him to help you feel safe and loved. God promises to be with you wherever you go!

THOUGHT OF THE DAY

When is a time you might feel lonely or afraid?

PRAY TODAY

Dear God, thank You for always being with me. Please help me remember You when I feel afraid or lonely. Amen.

PUTTING OTHERS FIRST

"So you want first place? Then take the last place. Be the servant of all."

MARK 9:35B MSG

This Bible verse doesn't seem to make sense. It says if you want to be first, you should be last! But Jesus isn't talking about winning a race or getting the highest grade on a test. He's talking about loving each other.

In God's kingdom, helping others is what is most important. Look around, who feels left out? Is there someone who needs a friend? Jesus says that when you help someone else, you are doing a good thing by serving them. And that makes you a winner! Jesus is looking for people who put others first.

THOUGHT OF THE DAY

How can you put someone else first today?

PRAY TODAY

Dear God, please help me to see who needs a friend today. Then help me to put them first. Amen.

YES, YOU CAN!

"For I am about to do something new. See, I have already begun! Do you not see it?"

ISAIAH 43:19A NLT

Do you like to try new things? Not everyone does! Sometimes it feels scary to try a new game, play with new friends, learn a new instrument, or even just tell someone about a new idea. God says you don't need to feel that way, because anything is possible when you have faith in Him! That doesn't mean you will be instantly perfect at everything you try. It means you can trust God to help you work hard, learn from your mistakes, and grow in confidence. When you depend on God's help, nothing can stop you!

THOUGHT OF THE DAY

What's something new you want to try?

PRAY TODAY

Dear God, sometimes I feel scared or embarrassed to try new things. Please help me remember to trust in Your help! Amen.

A MAP TO GOD

Jesus answered, "I am the way and the truth and the life. No one comes to the Father except through me."

JOHN 14:6 NIV

For a long time, people wondered what God was like. They wanted to get to know Him better, but they didn't know how. Then one day, God sent Jesus.

Jesus was God walking on earth! When Jesus came, no one had to wonder what God was like anymore—they could follow Him around! And you can do that too. When you feel like God is hard to understand, remember Jesus' life. He helped people who were different from Him, shared what He had, and loved everyone. Following Jesus closely is the best way to get close to God!

THOUGHT OF THE DAY

Jesus is like a secret passage to God's heart!

PRAY TODAY

Dear God, thank You for sending Jesus so I can understand You better and love You even more! Amen.

WORSHIP ALL THE TIME

Oh come, let us worship and bow down; let us kneel before the LORD, our Maker!

PSALM 95:6 ESV

Some people think they have to be in a church to worship God. But did you know that you can worship God wherever you are? Worshipping means using whatever you have, wherever you are, to honor and please God. You can worship God at the park by treating others the way God wants you to. You can worship God at home by being a helper and respecting your parents. You can worship God anywhere when you pray and sing and give thanks for all the amazing things He has done! Take time to worship God every day.

THOUGHT OF THE DAY

Can you name two ways you will worship God today?

PRAY TODAY

Dear God, You are so wonderful. I love You and I want to please You today in all I do! Amen.

MORE ISN'T BETTER

Don't be obsessed with getting more material things. Be relaxed with what you have.

HEBREWS 13:5 MSG

It is not wrong to want things—toys, clothes, fun times. But have you ever noticed that as soon as you get something you want, you start thinking about having something more? The Bible says that when we always want more, it's hard to be relaxed or happy with what we have. One way to be happier is to be thankful for what you already have. Then share what you have with others. Be creative! Find new ways to use something you have instead of always looking for something new. More isn't always better!

THOUGHT OF THE DAY

What are some new, creative ways you can use what you already have?

PRAY TODAY

Dear God, thank You for giving me so much. Please help me to be happy with what I have. Amen.

PLAY YOUR PART

And above all these put on love, which binds everything together in perfect harmony.

COLOSSIANS 3:14 ESV

When everyone in an orchestra plays their part on their instrument, the orchestra sounds beautiful. They are playing in harmony. When everyone on a team or in a family or in a classroom does their part, they are working in harmony. The team plays well. The family gets along. The classmates learn more. It's important to work and play in harmony with others. But that takes love. We need to learn to love each other and then celebrate our differences. No one can do every part, but when we each do our own part, everyone succeeds!

THOUGHT OF THE DAY

What part do you play in your family or classroom?

PRAY TODAY

Thank You, Lord, for making each person special. Please help me to do my part well so we can work together in harmony! Amen.

TRUE LOVE

My children, our love should not be only words and talk. Our love must be true love. And we should show that love by what we do.

1 JOHN 3:18 ICB

Love is more than just words. After all, if you say you love someone, then refuse to help or never share what you have, do you think they will believe your words are true? No! You have to show your love as well as speak it. God shows His love for us through good gifts like His beautiful world and His peace and joy. You can show love for your family by helping without being asked. You can love your friends by encouraging them and cheering when they do well. Find ways to show true love each day with words and actions.

THOUGHT OF THE DAY

What are some ways you can show true love today?

PRAY TODAY

Thank You, God, for loving me. Please help me show my love to others by what I do each day. Amen.

YOUR HELPER

If you don't know what you're doing, pray to the Father. He loves to help.

JAMES 1:5 MSG

Maybe you can name lots of dinosaurs or spell some long words. You might be able to sing well or solve puzzles quickly. But there are probably other things that aren't so easy for you. That's OK! No one is great at everything, and it takes time to learn. But don't give up and try not to get frustrated—you have an amazing Friend who would love to help you! When you are struggling to learn something new, talk to God. He can help you understand hard things and find new ways to solve problems.

THOUGHT OF THE DAY

What are you having a hard time learning? Why not ask God to help you?

PRAY TODAY

Dear God, thank You for being so wise. Please help me learn the things You want me to know. Amen.

POWERFUL PRAYERS

First of all, I ask you to pray for everyone. Ask God to help and bless them all, and tell God how thankful you are for each of them.

1 TIMOTHY 2:1 CEV

Do you ever feel like you are too small or too young to do anything important? Here's a secret—you can do wonderful things by praying for others. It doesn't matter how old you are or even how much you know. God hears your prayers, and He has all the power in the universe! He promises to hear your prayers for others and to use His power to help and bless them. You may be young, but when you put your faith in God, your prayers plus God's power make wonderful things happen!

THOUGHT OF THE DAY

Who will you pray for today?

PRAY TODAY

Dear God, thank You for always hearing my prayers and for using Your power to answer them. Amen.

COUNT ON GOD'S LOVE

And so we know the love that God has for us, and we trust that love.

1 JOHN 4:16A ICB

When Bible writers tell us about God's love they use a lot of big words, like *steadfast, everlasting*, and *unconditional*. Together, those words mean that God's love isn't going anywhere. You can count on God to love you every day, no matter what, forever. That's pretty amazing! Everything else in the world changes. People change and grow, seasons change each year, stars burn out or get bigger—you might even change your mind several times a day! But God never changes. He has always loved you, and He always will.

THOUGHT OF THE DAY

How does it feel to know God will always love you?

PRAY TODAY

Dear God, thank You for loving me every day, no matter what. I'm glad Your love never changes. Amen.

LET IT GO

When you are praying, if you are angry with someone, forgive him so that your Father in heaven will also forgive your sins.

MARK 11:25 NCV

Feeling angry can be uncomfortable. Maybe your face gets hot and your muscles tighten, or your tummy feels upset and you can't think straight. But God gives you a secret weapon to help you: forgiveness. God promises that forgiving others will actually help you feel better. That's because when you truly forgive, you agree to let go of what's making you angry. That may be hard, so ask for God's help. Hand over your angry feelings to God. Then you'll have room in your heart and mind to feel His peace.

THOUGHT OF THE DAY

Forgiveness pulls you away from anger and closer to God.

PRAY TODAY

Dear God, it's hard to forgive when I feel mad. Help me remember that forgiveness makes everyone feel better! Amen.

THE BEST KINDS OF FRIENDS

Friends come and friends go, but a true friend sticks by you like family.

PROVERBS 18:24 MSG

God gives us friends to share fun times with. But the Bible shows us that friendship can be even more than that. When King David was young, his best friend, Jonathan, hid him from a mean king who wanted to hurt David. In the book of Job, three friends showed up to support Job in a very sad time. And Jesus' disciple and friend Peter fought a soldier who came to arrest Jesus! It's important to have friends who stick around in good times and bad. Can you be that kind of friend today?

THOUGHT OF THE DAY

Who are some of your best friends?

PRAY TODAY

Dear God, friends are such wonderful gifts! Help me build strong friendships that last. Amen.

HEAVEN ON EARTH

"Your kingdom come. Your will be done on earth as it is in heaven."

MATTHEW 6:10 CSB

Did you know we can bring heaven to earth? The Bible tells us that in heaven, God's will is done. God's will means how God wants things to be.

We know God wants us to be kind, joyful, generous, and to live peacefully with everyone. So try it today! Look for ways to be kind, like helping without being asked, or inviting a new friend to play. Focus on the good parts of your day instead of things that went wrong. Share what you have and try to solve problems without fighting. When you do God's will, you bring heaven wherever you go.

THOUGHT OF THE DAY

God's will isn't hard—it's heavenly!

PRAY TODAY

Dear God, I want earth to look a little like heaven! Help me remember to speak and act like You want me to. Amen.

DON'T WAIT

"All of us must quickly carry out the tasks assigned us by the one who sent me, for there is little time left before the night falls and all work comes to an end."

JOHN 9:4 TLB

Laura promised to help Junior Asparagus learn to ride his scooter before his birthday. But she kept putting it off. One day she was busy playing ball. Another day she got interested in reading a book. When Junior reminded her of her promise, she said, "I'll do it later." Then it was Junior's birthday. He felt sad because he had wanted to ride his scooter all the way to the park for his party. Laura was sorry she had disappointed her friend. She decided that next time she made a promise to help someone she wouldn't wait. She would do it right away!

THOUGHT OF THE DAY

How can you help someone right now instead of waiting?

PRAY TODAY

Dear Jesus, thank You for always helping me. Please help me not to wait when I could be helping others. Amen.

ON GOD'S TEAM

For though we have never yet seen God, when we love each other God lives in us, and his love within us grows ever stronger.

1 JOHN 4:12 TLB

The Bible says that when you show love to someone, God is in you and working through you. And you two make a good team! Help your little brother learn something new? God's team in action! Share your lunch with a friend who forgot hers? Go Team God! Apologize for hurting a friend's feelings and ask to make things right? Another win! And don't worry about running out of love. God promises that the more you love others, the more love you'll have to give. When you're on His team, you can't lose!

THOUGHT OF THE DAY

How will you show love today?

PRAY TODAY

Dear God, I want to be on Your team. Let's show Your love to lots of people today! Amen.

CHOOSE TO WORK WELL

Work hard and cheerfully at all you do.

COLOSSIANS 3:23A TLB

Do you have chores at home? Do you have schoolwork you need to finish? Do you have to practice learning a sport or playing an instrument? You don't always get to choose the kinds of work you do, but you CAN choose how you do it. If you choose to complain, put it off, or not try very hard, the work can seem long and boring. But if you choose to focus, find creative ways to work, and do it well the first time, your work gets done better and faster—and it might even be fun! The Bible reminds us to choose to work well. Try it!

THOUGHT OF THE DAY

How can you work well today?

PRAY TODAY

Dear God, please help me do my work well, by working hard and cheerfully today. Amen.

HOW TO WAIT

I waited patiently for the Lord. He turned to me and heard my cry.

PSALM 40:1 NCV

When you're waiting for something, it's hard to be patient. You want to know what will happen. You might be excited or even a little bit afraid. Maybe you're worried about how things will work out or if they will happen the way you want. When you're waiting, it's always good to talk to God. Tell Him how you feel and what you're hoping for. God cares about you and He wants good things for you. As you talk to Him, you'll learn to trust Him more, and waiting can become easier. God can help you be patient.

THOUGHT OF THE DAY

What is something you're waiting for right now? Will you talk to God about it?

PRAY TODAY

Dear God, thank You for loving me. Help me wait patiently as You work out Your plans for me. Amen.

BE A TRUTH-TELLER

Since you put away lying, Speak the truth, each one to his neighbor, because we are members of one another.

EPHESIANS 4:25 HCSB

When you speak the truth, others learn they can trust you. They know you keep your promises. They know you won't tell a lie to cover up your mistakes. And they know they can count on you to do what you say. Truth-tellers make good friends. If you learn to be honest about little things, you will build the good habit of truth-telling. Then when big things come along, it will be easier for you to tell the truth about those things too. Make up your mind to be a truth-teller, then practice telling the truth every day!

THOUGHT OF THE DAY

How will you be a truth-teller today?

PRAY TODAY

Dear God, please help me to be a truth-teller so that others can trust me to be a good friend. Amen.

STAY CONNECTED

"Yes, I am the Vine; you are the branches. Whoever lives in me and I in him shall produce a large crop of fruit. For apart from me you can't do a thing."

JOHN 15:5 TLB

Have you ever picked apples? You can fill your bucket or basket in just a few minutes when the branches are loaded with delicious fruit. But if a branch breaks off the tree, it will never produce another apple. The branch must stay connected to the tree for apples to grow. The Bible says we are like those branches. We can do wonderful things when we stay connected to Jesus. You can do that by spending time reading your Bible, praying, and asking Jesus to help you every day. Then watch your "fruit" grow!

THOUGHT OF THE DAY

Name some ways you can connect with Jesus today.

PRAY TODAY

Dear Jesus, thank You for helping me to learn and grow. Please keep me close to You each day. Amen.

DO AND GROW

Be doers of the word, and not hearers only.

JAMES 1:22 NKJV

What if your teacher told you how to do a math problem, but you never did one yourself? What if your mom or dad showed how to ride a bike, but you never tried it? If you don't do something with all the things you learn, you won't grow! It's the same way when we hear God's words in the Bible. If we don't do what the words say, we won't grow as believers. God tells us to be kind, share, and help others. When we do these things, our faith grows stronger, and so does our friendship with God!

THOUGHT OF THE DAY

What is something God has told you to do?

PRAY TODAY

Dear God, thank You for telling me the right way to live. Please help me to do what You say. Amen.

WHEN YOU FEEL SAD

"Those who are sad now are happy. God will comfort them."

MATTHEW 5:4 ICB

Are there things that make you feel sad? Maybe a friend can't play. Maybe you broke a special toy or lost a favorite stuffy. Maybe someone you love is sick. Sometimes you just feel sad, and you can't even say why!

God knows that you have all kinds of feelings, and He wants to comfort you when you're sad. You can always tell Him how you're feeling or what you're thinking about. He also gives you people to love and share your feelings with. Talk to them too. Feelings come and go, but God's love and care is forever.

THOUGHT OF THE DAY

What helps you when you feel sad?

PRAY TODAY

Dear God, I'm so glad that You love me and care about my feelings. Thank You for comforting me when I feel sad. Amen.

YOU CAN DO IT

"Don't be afraid. Only believe."

MARK 5:36B HCSB

Have you ever tried to do something that seemed impossible or scary? Maybe you had to talk, sing, or play music in front of a group of people at church or school. Maybe you needed to tell the truth about something that you had done, and you were afraid you'd get into trouble. When you're afraid, Jesus says to believe in Him. He'll help you to do what you need to do because He loves you. He will calm your pounding heart and give you courage. With Jesus' help, you can do what seems impossible!

THOUGHT OF THE DAY

When were you afraid? What did you do?

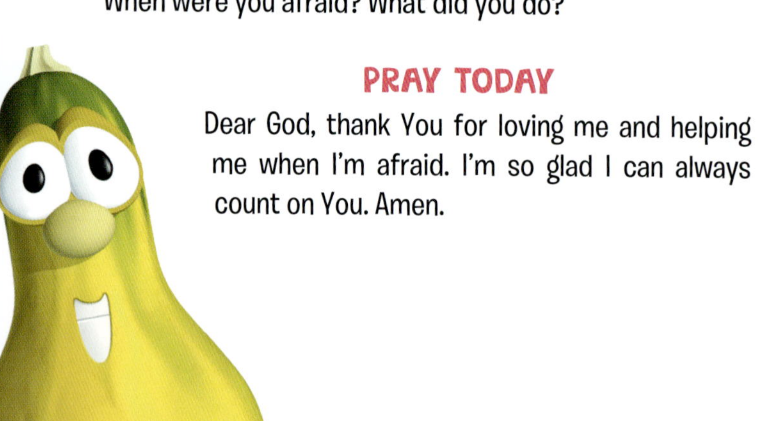

PRAY TODAY

Dear God, thank You for loving me and helping me when I'm afraid. I'm so glad I can always count on You. Amen.

GIVE GOOD THINGS

"Freely you have received; freely give."

MATTHEW 10:8B NIV

We each have been given so much. Not just presents on special occasions, but also kindness and love from friends and family. Why does God allow us to have good things we enjoy? The Bible says it's because God wants us to give good things to others! You can give some of your clothes, books, and toys to children who don't have much. You can give your time to help a neighbor. You can share your knowledge by helping a younger child learn something new. You have so much to give! How will you be a giver today?

THOUGHT OF THE DAY

Learning to give is the best way to live!

PRAY TODAY

Dear God, thank You for giving me so much! Please help me learn to be a joyful giver. Amen.

SHINE BRIGHTLY!

"You are the light of the world. A city situated on a hill cannot be hidden."

MATTHEW 5:14 HCSB

When you do kind things and make loving choices, people notice. It's like you have a bright flashlight inside you, powered by God's love. Whenever you do something like making a card for a neighbor, picking up garbage dropped in the park, letting a friend go first, helping your family at home, or inviting a younger kid to play, you shine your light. And that makes the world a little brighter for everyone. It might feel like you are doing small things, but you are making a big difference wherever you go!

THOUGHT OF THE DAY

How will you shine your light today?

PRAY TODAY

Dear God, I'm glad I can help others. Please help me shine brightly! Amen.

STAY CLOSE

I am offering you life or death, blessings or curses. Now, choose life! . . . To choose life is to love the LORD your God, obey him, and stay close to him.

DEUTERONOMY 30:19B–20A NCV

Decisions aren't always easy. Will you play soccer or take dance lessons? What cake is best for your birthday party? But one decision should be very clear: Choose to live your best life!

The Bible says that your best life happens when you stay close to God. So when you have a choice to make, ask yourself: Will this bring me closer to God or further away? Some choices won't make a difference, like choosing ham instead of turkey for your sandwich. But some choices will make a difference, like choosing to tell the truth or inviting a new kid to play. With God's help, your choices will deepen your friendship with Him.

THOUGHT OF THE DAY

When you choose God, you'll always choose right!

PRAY TODAY

Dear God, I want to stay close to You! Help me make the right choices when it matters most. Amen.

GOD'S COMFORT

When doubts filled my mind, your comfort gave me renewed hope and cheer.

PSALM 94:19 NLT

Are you ever afraid? Do you ever wonder about what will happen tomorrow? No person knows everything and no one can tell you exactly what will happen tomorrow. That's why it is so great to know God. He knows all things, and He is not afraid of anything! Whenever you feel afraid or worry about what will happen, you can ask God to help you. He promises to comfort you, to give you hope, and to cheer you up. God is more powerful than your fears and He loves you more than you can even imagine.

THOUGHT OF THE DAY

Give God your doubts and fears, and He will comfort you with hope.

PRAY TODAY

Dear God, thank You for loving me and comforting me when I'm afraid or worried. Amen.

WHY WISDOM?

Wisdom is more precious than rubies. Nothing you could want is equal to it.

PROVERBS 8:11 NCV

What's something you really, really want? How about . . . wisdom!

OK, it may not sound as exciting as a shiny new bike. But wisdom is one of God's best gifts. It means you always try to make good choices, and when you make mistakes, you learn from them and try again! A wise person remembers to thank God for what they have, and trusts that God will always provide—so they're not afraid to share. And they don't get stuck in angry arguments or jealous feelings. Doesn't that sound great? If you ask, God will help you grow in wisdom today!

THOUGHT OF THE DAY

Can you think of a time you made a wise choice? How did it feel?

PRAY TODAY

Dear God, You have the most wisdom of anyone. Please show me how I can be wise each day too. Amen.

ACT YOUR WORDS

Here's what you do: Live well, live wisely, live humbly. It's the way you live, not the way you talk, that counts.

JAMES 3:13B MSG

Can you think of a time someone broke a promise to you? Or has someone said they were a friend, then done something hurtful? The Bible says good words aren't very important without good actions. So when you say you'll do something, like clean up after dinner or put your clothes away, be sure you do it. And when you're friends with someone, be sure you act like it too—encourage them, listen to their ideas, and share what you have. When what you do matches what you say, people will see God's love in action!

THOUGHT OF THE DAY

Show the world you love Jesus by acting the way He would!

PRAY TODAY

Dear God, sometimes I forget to make my actions match my words. Please help me live well so people know I follow You. Amen.

A PURE HEART

Those with pure hearts shall become stronger and stronger.

JOB 17:9B TLB

Gold is a beautiful and precious metal. That makes it expensive, so people often mix it with other metals to make jewelry that doesn't cost as much. But if you ever see "24-karat gold," that means it's PURE—nothing added! And it's very valuable.

God wants you to have a pure heart—filled with nothing but Him! To have a pure heart, ask God to help you notice good things. Say thanks for what you have! Listen to wisdom from your teachers and parents. Ask forgiveness when you make mistakes. Pretty soon, you'll have a 24-karat heart for God!

THOUGHT OF THE DAY

Bible stories are full of people trying to have pure hearts. Read one today!

PRAY TODAY

Dear God, clean my heart and make it pure for You! Show me all the goodness You've made. Amen.

WISE VOICES

Listen carefully to wisdom; set your mind on understanding.

PROVERBS 2:2 NCV

The world is filled with voices. Toy makers tell you that if you buy their toys or games, you will be happy and popular. Clothing makers say that you will have lots of friends if you wear their brands. Their voices aren't always true or wise.

Our Bible verse today says to listen carefully. Your parents, good teachers, and friends who speak the truth are all voices that speak wisdom. You can trust them! Wise voices don't always say what you want to hear, but they do help you understand what's true. Listen to them. You'll be glad you did!

THOUGHT OF THE DAY

Who in your life can you trust to tell you the truth?

PRAY TODAY

Dear God, I trust in You. Please help me to listen to wise voices and to seek understanding. Amen.

A HAPPY HOME

"Honor your father and mother. Then you will live a long, full life in the land the LORD your God is giving you."

EXODUS 20:12 NLT

God gave us a list of good rules called the Ten Commandments. But only one of these rules comes with a promise. It's in today's verse! God says that life will be best when you are kind and respectful to your parents.

How does that work? It's simple! If you show respect to people, you'll get respect too. When you treat people with kindness, everyone is happier. When you get angry, choosing to speak calmly and listen well will help you make peace more easily. And when all this happens in a family, what a happy home you'll have!

THOUGHT OF THE DAY

Your family's a gift, so treat them with care. Be kind and respectful, and peace will be there!

PRAY TODAY

Dear God, thank You for my family. Please help me honor them every day. Amen.

FILLED WITH GOD

So we will not be afraid even if the earth shakes, or the mountains fall into the sea.

PSALM 46:2 NCV

It's normal to feel afraid sometimes. But the Bible says God is our protector. He is a safe place, and His love is forever. So when God fills your heart, there's no room for fear to live!

You can fill your heart with God by praying each day and learning Bible stories. God has been helping people feel brave since way back in Bible times! It might help to choose a song to sing each time you feel scared, like "Jesus Loves Me." When God's in your heart, scary feelings might creep in, but they can't stick around!

THOUGHT OF THE DAY

The words "fear not" appear 365 times in the Bible—that's once for every day of the year!

PRAY TODAY

Dear God, please fill my heart so fear has no place to stay. Amen!

BEING AFRAID

"Don't be afraid, for I am with you. Don't be discouraged, for I am your God. I will strengthen you and help you. I will hold you up with my victorious right hand."

ISAIAH 41:10 NLT

God knows that everyone gets afraid sometimes. Even grown-ups feel afraid! When a friend or family member is nearby and holds our hand, it helps calm our fears. Knowing that someone is with us makes us less afraid because we know we're not alone. But sometimes, there's no one nearby to hold our hand. That's when it is great to know that God says, "I will hold you up with my victorious right hand." When you're afraid, God is always right there with you. Trust Him to hold you and help you be brave.

THOUGHT OF THE DAY

When you fear, remember God is near!

PRAY TODAY

Thank You, God, for understanding that sometimes I'm afraid. Help me remember that You are always with me. Amen.

TURN ON THE LIGHT

Then Jesus spoke to them again, saying, "I am the light of the world. He who follows Me shall not walk in darkness, but have the light of life."

JOHN 8:12 NKJV

Imagine being stuck in a dark room. Would you feel confused? Scared? Now imagine you have a flashlight. You can see everything! The darkness cannot hide from you and your flashlight.

Bad feelings are like being in a dark room. When you're worried, angry, or jealous, it's hard to notice anything else. But when you think of Jesus' promises, it's like having a powerful flashlight. Remember His all-the-time love. Thank Him for the good gifts He's given you. Look for ways to show love to others. Dark feelings are no match for Jesus' light!

THOUGHT OF THE DAY

Nothing lights up your heart like remembering Jesus' love!

PRAY TODAY

Dear Jesus, I'm so glad You shine Your light everywhere. Help me remember Your love all the time! Amen.

WORDS THAT BUILD

When you talk, do not say harmful things. But say what people need—words that will help others become stronger. Then what you say will help those who listen to you.

EPHESIANS 4:29 ICB

People used to say, "Sticks and stones may break my bones, but words can never hurt me." If you've ever had your feelings hurt, you know that's not true! Words can feel just as painful as sticks and stones.

But the Bible says words can also make people stronger! When you pay attention and say what people need to hear, your words have amazing power. Does someone you know need to be encouraged or cheered up? Make sure you say those kinds of things! Then your words will help people up, not knock them down.

THOUGHT OF THE DAY

You can strengthen people everywhere when you choose your words with care.

PRAY TODAY

Dear God, help me notice what others need to hear. Then give me courage to say those things! Amen.

FIRST OF ALL, GOD

"But put God's kingdom first. Do what he wants you to do. Then all those things will also be given to you."

MATTHEW 6:33 NIRV

Do you have things to do before you can play? Maybe you have to finish your chores or homework or brush your teeth! Jesus told His disciples that the most important thing they should do is seek Him. Before they did anything at all, they needed to remember God and follow His ways.

Try to start each day with God first. Ask Him to help you make good choices, feel confident, or be a good friend. Praise Him for His goodness! Then trust Him to provide for you—He's promised He will!

THOUGHT OF THE DAY

When you put God first, you can handle whatever comes next!

PRAY TODAY

Dear God, I know You will keep Your promises to me. Help me to always put You first! Amen.

LOVE, NOT FEAR

There is no fear in love, but perfect love casts out fear. For fear has to do with punishment, and whoever fears has not been perfected in love.

1 JOHN 4:18A ESV

Sometimes fear is important, because it keep us safe. Feeling nervous around a growling dog is your body's way of telling you to give that dog some space! But other times, fear can keep you from doing great things. God has a solution for you. Fill your heart with love instead! When you love others, you feel more confident about making new friends or saying sorry. When you love yourself, you're less afraid of trying new things and making mistakes. And when you love God, you know He will always comfort and protect you, any time of the day or night.

THOUGHT OF THE DAY

God is love, so fill your heart with God!

PRAY TODAY

Dear God, please replace my fear with Your love, so I can be kind, confident, and comforted. Amen.

TRY GOING SECOND

"Greater love has no one than this: to lay down one's life for one's friends."

JOHN 15:13 NIV

God gives us an easy trick to being a great friend: let others go first. It's fun to be the line leader or the person who chooses what to play at recess. But try letting someone else go before you, and watch what happens. First, you'll make that person feel great. Everyone likes to feel important! Second, you might learn something new. Maybe your friend's funny idea will turn into your new favorite game! And third, YOU will feel great, because being kind is good for your heart. Ask God where you can go second today!

THOUGHT OF THE DAY

How does it feel to go first? Who can you give that feeling today?

PRAY TODAY

Dear God, please show me when I can give someone the gift of going first. Amen.

HIS LOVE IS ALL AROUND

"As the Father has loved Me, I have also loved you. Remain in My love."

JOHN 15:9 HCSB

Jesus' disciples traveled with Him for years and walked and talked with Him every day. You might think they would never feel upset about anything! But they got afraid and lonely and frustrated, just like you and me. Jesus reminded them that His love lasts forever! And if they remembered His wonderful, powerful love, they would have joy. Jesus has the same promise for you! When you feel upset, remember His love. Imagine sitting next to Jesus, just like His disciples did. Ask Him to comfort you. Even though you can't see Him, His love is always around.

THOUGHT OF THE DAY

Do you know the song "Jesus Loves Me"? Trying singing it each day to remind you of His love.

PRAY TODAY

Dear God, thank You for Your great love. I feel happy when I think of You. Amen.

FIRST PLACE

For God has not given us a spirit of fear and timidity, but of power, love, and self-discipline.

2 TIMOTHY 1:7 NLT

Do you feel like faster is better? Some people rush around because they're afraid to miss out on anything. But God has enough good things for everyone! Being first isn't important to God—He's interested in HOW you do things, not how fast you do them. Did you check to make sure your chores were done well? Did you walk carefully to get in line, so you didn't bump into anyone? Did you listen well to a friend's story before you told your own? It's not always easy to slow down or wait your turn. But when you do, you take first place in God's eyes!

THOUGHT OF THE DAY

Take your time and you will see: There's plenty of good for you and me!

PRAY TODAY

Dear God, I really like to be first. Please help me know when it's better to slow down and take turns. Amen.

SIGNS OF LOVE

But if we love one another, God dwells deeply within us, and his love becomes complete in us—perfect love!

1 JOHN 4:12B MSG

God loves you, and He leaves signs of His love all around you. He has given you a beautiful world. Just look at the sunset each night! He listens to your prayers. Think of how He gives you courage to try new things or calms your nervous heart when you're afraid. And most of all, He gives you other people to love. When you love others, you are feeling God's love inside you. God's love covers your whole life. No matter where you go, you can't get away from it!

THOUGHT OF THE DAY

We love others because God loved us first!

PRAY TODAY

Dear God, thank You for loving every part of me! Amen.

KEEP GOING!

Noah was another who trusted God. When he heard God's warning about the future, Noah believed him even though there was then no sign of a flood, and wasting no time, he built the ark and saved his family.

HEBREWS 11:7A TLB

The story of Noah is exciting. With an enormous ship, he saved his whole family—and two of every kind of animal—from a dangerous flood!

But for a long time, Noah's life wasn't very exciting at all. Building that ship was hard work. His friends and neighbors thought his work was silly—it sure didn't seem like a flood was coming soon! Noah was probably lonely and discouraged a lot of the time. But he decided to trust God anyway. He kept working, and when the flood came, he was ready—just like God had promised!

THOUGHT OF THE DAY

What's hard for you right now? Do you think God can help you keep going?

PRAY TODAY

Dear God, please help me trust You like Noah did. With Your help, I can do anything! Amen.

GOD'S NEXT STEPS

A man's heart plans his way, but the LORD determines his steps.

PROVERBS 16:9 HCSB

It's so much fun to think about what you'll do when you grow up. Will you become someone famous? Or invent something brand-new? Maybe you'll write books, or visit faraway places, or build houses, or have kids of your own! Everyone has different dreams. That's why the world is such an interesting place!

Do you have big dreams? Ask God to help you take steps toward your goal. You might not always know what to do next, but God does! He can help you become exactly the person He's made you to be.

THOUGHT OF THE DAY

Make big plans, and don't forget that God knows every best next step!

PRAY TODAY

Dear God, You know what I want in my heart. Please guide my steps so I can do big things for You! Amen.

GREAT TEACHERS

No one in this world always does right.

ECCLESIASTES 7:20 CEV

Everyone makes mistakes. Some mistakes are small—like hitting the wrong key when you're learning to play piano. Some mistakes are bigger, like when you hurt a friend's feelings. But all mistakes have one thing in common: They are great teachers! Wrong notes sound funny, and that helps you find the right ones instead. Wrong choices can make you feel icky, and that helps you make the right choice next time. Don't get discouraged! God doesn't expect you to be perfect. He loves to help you learn from your mistakes so you can grow wiser and kinder each day.

THOUGHT OF THE DAY

How does it feel when you make a mistake?

PRAY TODAY

Dear God, sometimes I feel frustrated when I make mistakes, but I'm so glad You can help me learn from them! Amen.

GOD ANSWERS

"Then you will call upon Me and go and pray to Me, and I will listen to you."

JEREMIAH 29:12 NKJV

God wants you to pray about anything. He wants to hear what you're wondering about, excited about, and worried about. And when you ask Him things, He promises to answer! But God's answers don't always come the way you expect. You can't always hear God, like you can hear another person. God can answer prayers by giving you new ideas, or by calming your nervous feelings, or even through wise words someone else says to you! Keep praying and ask for help to notice His answers when they come. Remember that He loves you and is always with you.

THOUGHT OF THE DAY

God loves to hear and answer your prayers.

PRAY TODAY

Dear God, I love to talk to You. Help me be patient while I wait for Your answers. Amen.

YOU ARE NEEDED

None of you should look out just for your own good. Each of you should also look out for the good of others.

PHILIPPIANS 2:4 NIRV

It's easy to notice when you need something. You've just moved in, and you'd like a friend. You're feeling sad and could use a laugh. You're hungry—you need a snack! But do you also notice when others need your help?

God wants us to pay attention to others too. Is your little sister grumpy? She might feel better if you play with her. Did your friend forget a snack? Try sharing yours! It takes practice, but caring for others is how we build healthy families and friendships. It's how God designed us! And it feels great too.

THOUGHT OF THE DAY

Look for one way you can help someone today. Then give it a try!

PRAY TODAY

Dear God, I'm so glad I have loving friends and family. Please show me how I can be a helper to them. Amen.

LET'S SING!

Sing to the Lord *a new song; sing to the* Lord*, all the earth. Sing to the* Lord *and praise his name; every day tell how he saves us.*

PSALM 96:1–2 NCV

The Veggies love to sing songs—happy songs and silly songs, songs that tell stories and songs that make you want to dance! Do you know who else loves songs? God does! He loves to hear His children singing and making music. Singing is a great way to remind ourselves how much God loves us. Have you ever learned fun songs at Sunday school, church camp, or Vacation Bible School? Why not sing them? Or make up your own! It's a fun way to tell God know how much we love Him and how glad we are that He loves us too!

THOUGHT OF THE DAY

What song would you like to sing to God?

PRAY TODAY

Dear God, thank You for loving me. Please fill my heart with songs I can sing to You! Amen.

A SPEEDY ESCAPE

Run from temptations that capture young people. Always do the right thing.

2 TIMOTHY 2:22A CEV

Are you ever tempted to do something you know isn't right? A friend might want you to disobey the rules at school. Perhaps you feel tempted to ignore or make fun of someone. You might want to take something that doesn't belong to you. Everyone faces temptations, but the Bible says it's important to do the right thing instead. And sometimes, that means leaving the place or the people who are tempting you. God can help! Ask God to show you how to make a speedy escape to stop from doing the wrong thing!

THOUGHT OF THE DAY

Think of two ways you could make a speedy escape the next time you are tempted to do the wrong thing.

PRAY TODAY

Dear God, will You help me escape from temptation? I want to do the right thing instead. Amen.

GOD KEEPS HIS PROMISES

"But your name shall be Abraham, for I have made you the father of a multitude of nations."

GENESIS 17:5B ESV

Thousands of years ago, God told a man named Abram to take his family and move away from his homeland. Abram didn't know where he was going, but he trusted God. Abram and his wife, Sarai, had no children, but after they obeyed God and moved to a new place, God gave them an amazing promise. He changed Abram's name to Abraham and Sarai's name to Sarah, and He told them they would be the parents of "a multitude of nations." It seemed impossible, but God did what He promised. God always keeps His promises. You can trust what He says.

THOUGHT OF THE DAY

What God promises, He will do. He's faithful to me and you!

PRAY TODAY

Dear God, thank You for promising to be with me always. I'm so glad You always keep Your promises. Amen.

LEARNING TO FORGIVE

Then Peter came to him and asked, "Lord, how often should I forgive someone who sins against me? Seven times?" "No, not seven times," Jesus replied, "but seventy times seven!"

MATTHEW 18:21-22 NLT

When someone hurts your feelings or ruins something that is special to you, how do you feel? Angry? Sad? Upset? It is normal to feel that way, but it is not good to stay angry or upset. When Peter asked Jesus a question about this, Jesus said that it is important to forgive others. That means we give up the right to get even or hurt someone back. When we choose to forgive, we are obeying Jesus and learning to be more like Him. Jesus always forgives us, and He wants us to learn to forgive others too.

THOUGHT OF THE DAY

How do you feel when someone forgives you? Who is someone you need to forgive?

PRAY TODAY

Dear God, I'm so glad You always forgive me. Please help me forgive others, even when it's hard. Amen.

GOD'S AMAZING GIFT

"For this is how God loved the world: He gave his one and only Son, so that everyone who believes in him will not perish but have eternal life."

JOHN 3:16 NLT

God created a beautiful world for us to live in. But He also wants us to live with Him forever, so He did something even more wonderful. God sent His Son, Jesus, to earth to show us how to live and love one another. Jesus lived a perfect life, and after He died, God raised Him from the dead. Now Jesus lives with God in heaven, and God shows His great love for us by promising that anyone who trusts in Jesus can also live with Him in heaven forever. What an amazing gift!

THOUGHT OF THE DAY

What did God do to show His amazing love for us?

PRAY TODAY

Dear God, thank You for loving me so much. Please help me learn to love and trust in Jesus more each day. Amen.

GOD'S UNIQUE GIFTS

Something from the Spirit can be seen in each person, to help everyone.

1 CORINTHIANS 12:7 ICB

Do you ever wish you could be like someone else? Guess what? God never wishes that. He loves you exactly the way you are, and He gave you special gifts that are just for you! No one else cares, smiles, jokes, or helps exactly the way you do. No one's brain works the same way yours does, and no one else has your creative ideas. Think about what you like to do and then ask God how you can grow those gifts and interests. You may discover that your unique gifts can do big things!

THOUGHT OF THE DAY

God's great gifts to you and me make earth a super place to be!

PRAY TODAY

Dear God, please help me be thankful for the gifts You gave me. How can I use them today? Amen.

BIGGER THAN THE STORM

So we will not be afraid even if the earth shakes, or the mountains fall into the sea.

PSALM 46:2 NCV

Have you ever been through a big thunderstorm? The rain splashes down, lightning flashes, and thunder booms so loudly it can make your windows shake! Sometimes the wind blows down tree branches, and sometimes all the lights go out.

It can feel scary to be in the middle of a storm. But did you know that God is even more powerful? He made everything, so He is greater than any of it! Next time you feel scared, whether from a big storm outside, a small worry in your heart, or anything in between, remember that God can handle anything!

THOUGHT OF THE DAY

Thunder crashes, lightning flashes, but God is always here with you.

PRAY TODAY

Dear God, sometimes I feel scared. Help me remember that I'm never alone, and You are always in control. Amen.

WHAT WOULD GOD DO?

Don't be like the people of this world, but let God change the way you think. Then you will know how to do everything that is good and pleasing to him.

ROMANS 12:2 CEV

Why is it so hard to make good choices sometimes? Because no one's perfect! We all get mad, tired, shy, or even just hungry—and those feelings can lead us to make less-than-great decisions. The good news is, God loves to help you. Try this trick: Imagine what God would do in your place.

God's thoughts aren't our thoughts, so it takes some practice. You could make up a short prayer to say any time you need a little extra help. Something as simple as "God, what would You do?" can build a great habit for making great choices!

THOUGHT OF THE DAY

Try to think like God at least one time today. See what happens!

PRAY TODAY

Dear God, please help me think about You all day so I can make the choices You would make! Amen.

JOYFUL HELP

Do everything without complaining and arguing.

PHILIPPIANS 2:14 NLT

Something wonderful about God is that He loves helping us. You don't have to argue or beg—helping you brings God joy!

You might not know it, but helping can bring you joy too. Think about a time you picked out a perfect birthday gift for your mom. How did you feel? Or what about a time you cheered up a friend who got hurt? Next time someone asks you to do something that feels boring or hard (chores, anyone?), remember another time it felt great to help out. Then say yes without complaining. You might be surprised by joy!

THOUGHT OF THE DAY

Try helping without being asked today. It's a fun surprise!

PRAY TODAY

Dear God, sometimes I really don't feel like helping out. Help me make it fun and joyful, like it is for You! Amen.

GOD IS ALWAYS THERE

Since God assured us, "I'll never let you down, never walk off and leave you," we can boldly quote, "God is there, ready to help; I'm fearless no matter what. Who or what can get to me?"

HEBREWS 13:5-6 MSG

Sometimes friends or family can't be with you. Maybe a parent needs to take a trip, or your friend is on vacation. You might spend the night in a hospital or go to camp. At those times, you might feel alone or even a little afraid. But here's some great news! God says He will never leave you. You can talk to Him out loud, pray to Him silently, even sing a song to Him! You can ask Him to help you be brave and to feel less lonely. He is always with you, no matter where you are.

When do you need to remember that God is with you?

PRAY TODAY

Dear God, I am so glad that You promise to always be with me. Thank You for never leaving me. Amen.

COPY JESUS' ATTITUDE

Make your own attitude that of Christ Jesus.

PHILIPPIANS 2:5 HCSB

Your attitude is the way you show your feelings by how you act. When you're feeling angry, you might slam a door or throw a toy to show your attitude. When you're feeling upset, you might cry or hide. When you're happy, you might smile and skip or bounce around. Jesus showed His attitude of love by being kind, forgiving others, listening to people, and helping them. The Bible says we should try to have the same attitude as Jesus. How can you show a loving attitude to your friends and family?

THOUGHT OF THE DAY

What will you do today to show a loving and caring attitude?

PRAY TODAY

Dear God, sometimes my attitude isn't like Yours. Please help me to show a loving and caring attitude today. Amen.

GOD NEVER CHANGES

"I have loved you with a love that lasts forever. I have kept on loving you with a kindness that never fails."

JEREMIAH 31:3B NIRV

Things and people change. Babies grow up. Our toys wear out. Clothes get dirty or torn. Pets get older. Things in our homes break. Even mountains and rivers change over time. But do you know who *never* changes? God!

God never changes His mind or breaks a promise. God will never stop loving you. He will always be kind and caring. He is always ready to forgive you when you ask Him to. It's great to know that God is always the same. You can count on Him.

THOUGHT OF THE DAY

Name three ways you have changed since you were small.

PRAY TODAY

Dear God, I am so glad that You never change and that I can always count on You to love and care for me. Amen.

SHARE SOME SMILES

Smiling faces make you happy, and good news makes you feel better.

PROVERBS 15:30 GNT

Have you ever played a game where you and a friend stare at each other and you try not to smile? Before long, someone cracks a smile and then the other person ends up grinning too. Smiles are catching! Wear a smile and you will find that you feel happier and so do others!

Another way to cheer someone up is to share some good news. Maybe your pet did something funny, or you learned a new joke. Is there something fun planned at school, church, or in your neighborhood? Share it! Good news makes everyone feel better!

THOUGHT OF THE DAY

How will you share some smiles today?

PRAY TODAY

Dear God, thank You for friends who make me smile. Help me remember to share some smiles with others today. Amen.

KNOW IT BY HEART

MOM OR DAD, HELP YOUR DAUGHTER MEMORIZE THIS VERSE AND TALK TO HER ABOUT WHAT IT MEANS.

Trust the Lord with all your heart.
Don't depend on your own understanding.

PROVERBS 3:5 ICB

KNOW IT BY HEART

MOM OR DAD, HELP YOUR DAUGHTER MEMORIZE THIS VERSE AND TALK TO HER ABOUT WHAT IT MEANS.

Whatever you do, do everything for the glory of God.

1 CORINTHIANS 10:31B CSB

KNOW IT BY HEART

MOM OR DAD, HELP YOUR DAUGHTER MEMORIZE THIS VERSE
AND TALK TO HER ABOUT WHAT IT MEANS.

The heavens declare
the glory of God;
the skies proclaim
the work of his hands.

PSALM 19:1 NIV

KNOW IT BY HEART

MOM OR DAD, HELP YOUR DAUGHTER MEMORIZE THIS VERSE AND TALK TO HER ABOUT WHAT IT MEANS.

He has shown you, O man,
what is good;
And what does the LORD
require of you
But to do justly,
To love mercy,
And to walk humbly
with your God?

MICAH 6:8 NKJV

KNOW IT BY HEART

MOM OR DAD, HELP YOUR DAUGHTER MEMORIZE THIS VERSE
AND TALK TO HER ABOUT WHAT IT MEANS.

We love because God first loved us.

1 JOHN 4:19 ICB

KNOW IT BY HEART

MOM OR DAD, HELP YOUR DAUGHTER MEMORIZE THIS VERSE AND TALK TO HER ABOUT WHAT IT MEANS.

Jesus said to him, "I am the way, and the truth, and the life. No one comes to the Father except through me."

JOHN 14:6 ESV

KNOW IT BY HEART

MOM OR DAD, HELP YOUR DAUGHTER MEMORIZE THIS VERSE AND TALK TO HER ABOUT WHAT IT MEANS.

Be strong and brave.
Don't be afraid of them and
don't be frightened, because the
LORD your God will go with you.
He will not leave you or forget you."

DEUTERONOMY 31:6 NCV

KNOW IT BY HEART

MOM OR DAD, HELP YOUR DAUGHTER MEMORIZE THIS VERSE AND TALK TO HER ABOUT WHAT IT MEANS.

In the beginning God created the heavens and the earth.

GENESIS 1:1 NLT

KNOW IT BY HEART

MOM OR DAD, HELP YOUR DAUGHTER MEMORIZE THIS VERSE AND TALK TO HER ABOUT WHAT IT MEANS.

The grass withers, the flower fades,
but the word of our God stands forever.

ISAIAH 40:8 NASB

KNOW IT BY HEART

MOM OR DAD, HELP YOUR DAUGHTER MEMORIZE THIS VERSE
AND TALK TO HER ABOUT WHAT IT MEANS.

"Come to me, all of you who are tired and have heavy loads, and I will give you rest."

MATTHEW 11:28 NCV

KNOW IT BY HEART

MOM OR DAD, HELP YOUR DAUGHTER MEMORIZE THIS VERSE AND TALK TO HER ABOUT WHAT IT MEANS.

My dear brothers, always be willing to listen and slow to speak. Do not become angry easily.

JAMES 1:19 ICB